DEAR MRS. NOAH

For Jean ~
Joy
Roberta Dawson

DEAR MRS. NOAH

LETTERS TO UNNAMED WOMEN OF THE BIBLE

ROBERTA M. DAMON

CROSSLINK PUBLISHING

Dear Mrs. Noah: Letters to Unnamed Women of the bible
Copyright © 2017 by Roberta M. Damon.

CrossLink Publishing
www.crosslinkpublishing.com

ISBN 978-1-63357-102-0

Library of Congress Control Number: 2016963029

ILLUSTRATIONS BY MELISSA DAMON

ENDORSEMENTS

"The significance of a story is not measured by the amount of ink required to print it, but by it impact on the heart of the one who reads it. Roberta takes the stories of unnamed women in the Bible and gives them a name and a voice that speaks to our own struggles and hopes. The passion of the God who relentlessly pursued His people on the pages of Scripture is still relentlessly pursuing us. He knew them... and He knows us, by name."

Beverly L. Carroll, Author *God Chooses People Like You*

"Imaginatively entering into the Biblical text using her knowledge of historical context and family psychology, Dr. Damon creates an evocative text for recognizing issues of faith, doubt, belief, identity, shame, and affirmation in both historical and contemporary people. This book is a treasure for personal reading and small group study."

Phyllis Rodgerson Pleasants Terrieri,
John F. Loftis Professor of Church History (retired)
Baptist Theological Seminary at Richmond

"With gentle skill and keen insight, Roberta Damon sheds light on more than thirty previously unnamed women of the Bible. The stories come to life with the illustrations provided by her talented granddaughter, Melissa Damon. This book can be used for personal devotions or in group discussion."

Daniel G. Bagby, Emeritus Professor Pastoral Care,
Baptist Theological Seminary at Richmond

"Roberta Damon creatively weaves individual testimonies of unnamed Biblical women into a larger narrative. She channels the spirit of the unnamed, tells their stories, and gives validity to their personhood. This thought provoking work raises women to a higher level."

Valerie Carter, Executive Director/Treasurer,
Women's Missionary Union of Virginia

"Their qualities of character and extraordinary deeds gave more than thirty nameless women a place in the Bible. They come alive in Damon's letters, her granddaughter's illustrations, and through questions that touch our hearts and help us ponder our own faith. You will want to add this stimulating book to your resources for personal devotion or group conversation."

Michael Clingenpeel, Pastor emeritus, River Road Church,
Baptist, Richmond, Virginia

"In your reading of the Bible, have you ever heard of Darlene, Felicity, Sally, Kara or Marvella?

You have met them, but they were previously unnamed. Roberta Damon skillfully and engagingly writes with a counselor's insight, a believer's trust, and an educator's knowledge as she incorporates the known with the educated guess. This book will appeal to girls and women, but it is valuable for boys and men."

Fred Anderson, Christian writer and Executive Director of the Virginia Baptist Historical Society and the Center for Baptist Heritage & Studies at the University of Richmond

"*Dear Mrs. Noah* is an insider's story of one who stepped into the shoes of unnamed women of the Bible. Roberta Damon wondered, imagined, and conversed with more than thirty Biblical women and gave them names. In so doing, she conferred on them the noble title, 'Daughters of God.'"

Bill O'Brien, Executive Director, Gaston Christian Center, Dallas

Founding Director of the Global Center, Samford University

"Roberta Damon is a Christian, teacher, missionary, therapist, writer, public speaker and friend. Her knowledge of Scripture, deep insights and perception of people made this book a natural for her. I have, with, joy, observed her leading therapy groups in more than twenty *Healthy Wellness Retreats for Ministers and Spouses* sponsored by the Ministering to Ministers Foundation for over two decades. I highly recommend this book for personal reading and group study."

Charles Chandler, Executive Director and Founder, Ministering to Ministers

"Roberta Damon has given us a treasure which inspires both thought and reflection about what our own names might mean. I am delighted that she has brought life to some of the overlooked women in the Bible and connected them so thoughtfully to our lives today."

Betty Ann Dillon, Clinical Psychologist (retired)

"Roberta Damon brings unique insight into the lives of unnamed women of the Bible. Her extensive research, thoughtful presentation, and subtle humor will delight and inform the reader. I commend this accessible study for groups or personal use.

Ronald L. Dubois, Marriage and Family Counselor

"Roberta: German, feminine of Robert; bright fame

Roberta Damon is living up to her name. She is brilliant and creative in telling the stories of unnamed women in Scripture. She raises them up and makes them visible. They become known when they are named."

Beverley Buston, Clinical Psychologist

"Roberta Damon reads the Biblical text like an X-Ray machine. She sees beneath the surface, and shows us the thoughts, motives, and the complex personalities of the unnamed women who populate the pages of Scripture."

James G. Somerville, Pastor, First Baptist Church, Richmond, Virginia

DEDICATION

To all the women who have borne the children,
fed the hungry,
washed the dishes—
And have not kept silent in church.

TABLE OF CONTENTS

FOREWORD

WE ARE LAZY BIBLE STUDENTS. How many times have we read the stories of women in the Bible with neither awareness nor question about the absence of their names? Naming is the first act of identity. Yet, we have blithely ignored this vacuum in Biblical narratives related to accounts of women without their names. That omission is no longer necessary, or permissible, due to Roberta Damon's incisive, engaging study that reviews the stories of unnamed women in the Bible and gives to each of them a name with explicit reasons for the choice. *Dear Mrs. Noah: Letters to Unnamed Women of the Bible*, charms and enlightens readers with the author's insights transmitted through Biblical and cultural knowledge. The stories she weaves come from a depth of Biblical study and understanding that interprets from the close attention to details which both reveal and create character. The rhetorical structure of letters provides an intimate conversation with each woman and presents to the reader an unthreatened proximity to them. Because of Damon's equally exact understanding of the cultures where her subjects lived, she instructs readers at the same time she engages them. We can take comfort from the names Biblical women now have through the imagination and writing skill of the author. We can meet each woman as we read her story and address her by the name through which Damon has given her identity.

Dear Mrs. Noah: Letters to Unnamed Women of the Bible, in conversational style, yet deep in Biblical and cultural truth, gives serious students who want to understand the deep implication for women to be made in the image of God a new assessment of the faithfulness between God and the feminine half of His creation.

Gladys S. Lewis, Professor emeritus of English,
University of Central Oklahoma, Writer,
Speaker, Churchwoman

INTRODUCTION

WHAT'S IN A NAME? SHAKESPEARE'S Romeo may have been correct in saying, "A rose by any other name may smell as sweet," but "rose" means a particular flower and differentiates this flower from that one, so that everyone will understand a rose is a rose and not a sunflower. The name identifies and gives identity. A name possesses power, and something powerful occurs in the act of naming. In calling a person's name, one has power over that person. If you hear your name called, your attention is immediately engaged.

In both the Old and New Testaments, people's names had special meaning. Jacob meant "supplanter." And when God renamed him "Israel" (soldier of God), it was because his entire life and character had been changed. When Naomi ("pleasant') returned to her own country after the death of her husband and sons, she asked that her old friends call her "Mara" (bitter). Abram (a high father) became "Abraham" (father of a great multitude), and Sarai ("contentious") became "Sarah" ("princess"). In the New Testament, Saul gets the name of Paul after his life-changing experience on the road to Damascus. In a sense, this change in names is true of all of us. When we experience the living Christ, our lives and our characters are changed. In a real way, we are named anew. We become "Christian," from the Greek: "Little Christ." Now, there is a name to emulate.

The name is one of the first things parents think about when they know a child will be born to them. Even abandoned babies are often given a name by their birth mothers. This act of naming provides evidence that a child without a name is a nobody.

Across the multiple centuries and cultures of what we often lump together as "Bible Times," we find many women who are not named. That does not mean they did not have names, but rather, the names were not recorded as part of their story. We know these women by some identifying phrase: "the woman with the issue of blood," "the woman at the well," or "the widow's mite." Or, we identify them in relationship to a male relative: "Job's wife," "Lot's wife," "Peter's mother-in-law."

We encounter many men in the Bible who are not named—the ten lepers, the blind man of Bethsaida, the Greeks who came to Jesus, but considering the genealogical records in the Bible, we remember that Israel was patriarchal. Mentioned in "the begats" were sons of fathers through multiple generations. In the genealogies of Jesus, given by Luke and Matthew, only four women, besides Mary, were called by name: Rahab, the prostitute; Ruth, the foreigner; Tamar, the rape victim; and Bathsheba, the adulteress.

On these pages you will not find Mary Magdalene, Phoebe, or Dorcas. They were called by name. You will find here, however, other Bible women whose stories are familiar but whose names we do not know. Here they receive names—suitable names—that give their stories greater resonance, providing space for reflection and adoption of meaning that enhances our names and stories.

THE WOMAN BENT OVER DOUBLE

On a Sabbath, Jesus was teaching in one of the synagogues, and a woman was there who had been crippled by a spirit for eighteen years. She was bent over and could not straighten up at all. When Jesus saw her, he called her forward and said unto her, "Woman, you are set free from your infirmity." Then he put his hands on her, and immediately she straightened up and praised God. Indignant because Jesus had healed on the Sabbath, the synagogue ruler said to the people, "There are six days for work, so come and be healed on those days and not on the Sabbath." The Lord answered him, "You hypocrite! Doesn't each of you on the Sabbath untie his ox or donkey from the stall and lead it to give it water? Then should not this woman, a daughter of Abraham, whom Satan has kept bound for eighteen long years, be set free on the Sabbath day from what bound her?" When he said this, all his opponents were humiliated, but the people were delighted with all the wonderful things he was doing.

Luke 13:10–17

Dear Little Woman,

ICANNOT IMAGINE WHAT YOU suffered for eighteen years. Not to be able to stand erect has all kinds of implications—physical pain, emotional distress, the humiliation of being overlooked and discounted. I understand that in your culture, physical illness indicated punishment for sin—a double indictment. In my culture, handicapped people are perceived in a similar way. People tend to avert their eyes and avoid contact with such people. I suppose it has to do with the helplessness we feel in the presence of a catastrophic condition.

You are amazing. How much did it cost you in energy and determination to be in the synagogue that day when Jesus saw you? And isn't it astonishing that Jesus saw you—not just with his eyes, but with his great heart? I do know enough about your culture to know that a man was not to look at a woman—not to speak to a woman. And, certainly, a man was never to touch a woman in public. Don't look. Don't speak. Don't touch. Jesus did all three. He always was unafraid to do things which scandalized the prim and proper—the keepers of the letter of the Law who were so absolutely convinced of their own righteousness.

After eighteen years of being "bound by Satan," according to Jesus, the miracle came that you had asked of God all that miserable time. When Jesus touched you—laid his hands on you—what must you have felt! An immediate liberation—a jolt of power—a sudden realization that you were made whole, healthy, straight—my soul, what a glorious experience! Your reaction was to glorify God. I can imagine your jumping for joy and then bowing yourself in deep gratitude as you kissed his feet and his dear hands. How could you not?

And then, the ruler of the synagogue showed up complaining and quoting scripture. He missed it, didn't he—the miracle of healing—the rejoicing—the gratitude. Poor blind man! Does there always have to be someone to rain on the parade? Jesus called him a hypocrite—and he was, of course. Jesus called you "daughter of Abraham." Do you know that nowhere else in all of scripture was anyone else ever called "daughter of Abraham?" It's true. "Sons of Abraham," "children of Abraham," "seed of Abraham," but only you were called "daughter of Abraham"—worthy to be healed on the Sabbath day.

Did you notice how his enemies slithered away in shame? Did you see how the other people rejoiced because of the wonderful things Jesus did?

When Jesus healed you that day, you could stand tall. You could hold your head up. You had a new identity. I don't know your real name, but I shall call you "Gloria." Praise God from Whom all blessings flow.

Gloria—"Praise"

REFLECTING

What healing would you request of Jesus if you found yourself physically in his presence?

You must know people who are like the ruler of the synagogue in this story. Who are they? How have they wounded you? Are they likely to ask your forgiveness? If they never ask you for forgiveness, how will you deal with them?

How do you define yourself? From what source comes your identity?

What makes you able to hold your head up?

Make a list of reasons to rejoice.

THE WIDOW'S MITE

As he looked up, Jesus saw the rich putting their gifts into the temple treasury. He also saw a poor widow put in two very small copper coins. "I tell you the truth," he said. "This poor widow has put in more than all the others. All these people gave their gifts out of their wealth; but she out of her poverty put in all she had to live on."

Luke 21:1–4

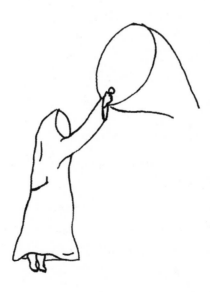

Dear Little Widow,

HAD YOU LIVED IN MY century, you might well have gone back to school, learned a trade, taken a job and been able to take care of yourself. Living as you did in the first century, you were out of luck—no survivor's benefits or social security for you. Our system isn't perfect, but it's better than yours—having to have a father, a husband, or a son to look after you.

And what on earth were you thinking, taking the last pitiful little coins you had and giving them to the temple treasury? Surely, all those rich men showing off their wealth could have supplied the temple with all that was needed. Your little coins could not have helped much—not at the temple, and not when it came time for you to buy groceries.

If I close my eyes, I can picture the scene: the crowd gathers at the temple treasury waiting to see which lavishly dressed man will, with great ceremony, put into the offering more than anyone else. He approaches with much pomp—a false humility marking his countenance. He heaves the heavy metal coins against the metal of the receptacle. Metal on metal makes a cacophonous sound. The crowd cheers. The generous giver bows his head as if in obeisance to God, but he hears the crowd's tumultuous response. Smiling inwardly he goes his way, satisfied that he has given more than anyone else—and it was duly noted. He has done it to the approval of the temple crowd. And then, I can see you. You do not come with ceremony. You are shabbily dressed, and the crowd pays you no attention. The temple faithful are still commenting to each other what a wonderful thing it was that the rich man gave so much—sighing that one day, perhaps, they too, will be wealthy and able to give a substantial offering to the religious crowd's great cheers. Public recognition has its compensations. However, if public deeds are done for recognition, then the purpose and reward are served. You hold a different intention. Like Jesus' message in the Sermon on the Mount, your offering related to the acts of righteousness in almsgiving, prayer, and fasting should be in private, between the individual and God. So, you are not noticed. You are just a woman—a poor one at that—a widow—a triple deficit. What about you could possibly interest this crowd? You certainly have nothing of value to cast into the treasury. And so you toss in those pitiful little coins. The subdued "ping" they produce is an indication of your poverty. No one notices—or if they do, it is with irritation that you are holding up the line of wealthy givers. As you toss in your offering, you are well aware that you have nothing left for food. What in the world were you thinking? Did you have to give all of it? Couldn't you have kept something back for your supper? You have no money left! None!

Oh. Wait. Right. This wasn't about the money, was it? You wanted to give something to God. Actually, you wanted to give everything to God. Jesus saw your heart. You didn't care what the crowd noticed or didn't notice. You weren't there for them. What motivates a person to give everything—even when it means there is nothing left for food? Who would do such a thing? Only someone who loves God more than self—who gives to the last breath—who does it without hope of recognition. Love brought you to the temple treasury that day. Love— pure love.

I will name you Amadene. I like to think that some of those women who followed Jesus from Galilee brought you supper that evening. If you had lived in my time, the women in our church would have seen to it that you had food in your pantry. Women through all the ages have taken care of those in need. There is more than one way to love.

Amadene ... Feminine of Amadeus—Latin "Lover of God."

REFLECTING

What is most precious to you?

How are you affected by public opinion?

What do you think it means to give all you have?

Do you believe God is aware of our most secret desires for approval from others?

THE WOMAN WITH THE ISSUE OF BLOOD

A large crowd followed and pressed around him. And a woman was there who had been subject to bleeding for twelve years. She had suffered a great deal under the care of many doctors and had spent all she had, yet instead of getting better she grew worse. When she heard about Jesus, she came up behind him in the crowd and touched his cloak, because she thought "If I just touch his clothes, I will be healed." Immediately her bleeding stopped and she felt in her body that she was freed from her suffering. At once Jesus realized that power had gone out from him. He turned around in the crowd and asked, "Who touched my clothes?" "You see the people crowding against you," his disciples answered, "and yet you can ask, 'Who touched me?'" But Jesus kept looking around to see who had done it. Then the woman, knowing what had happened to her, came and fell at his feet and, trembling with fear, told him the whole truth. He said to her, "Daughter, your faith has healed you. Go in peace and be freed from your suffering."

Mark 5:24b–34

Dear One,

HOW TERRIBLE TO BE FOREVER known as the woman with the issue of blood. From the time of Moses, women were declared unclean after childbirth and at monthly cycles, and that always meant that she was a contaminant. If she sat on the same chair or bed with her husband, not only was she considered unclean, but so was he. That is, he was unfit to approach God in worship and had to submit to ritual cleansing before he was clean—worthy— before God. I don't have to remind you. You lived with the shame, the humiliation, every day for twelve years. Well, the doctors couldn't help you. Of course, they could take your money. How many worthless potions did they sell you? And with what hope did you swallow each one? How discouraged and how frantic did you become?

How did you hear of the Nazarene? Did you hear Him preach? Did you sit on a hillside while He taught? Did His reputation precede Him? Did you hear of Magdalene, now cured of seven devils? Did you hear Jesus had compassion on the widow from Nain and raised her son from the dead? Did you hear of the mad man of Gadera, now healed and in his right mind? How came you to be in the crowd that day? What made you think that by simply touching His robe you would be healed?

Well, you did it. And you were healed. I imagine you thought you could just slip away without anyone's being the wiser. But He knew. And when He asked, "Who touched me?" you knew you couldn't hide.

What did you think He was going to do—rescind the miracle? No wonder you trembled with fear.

I can only imagine what it must have been like to look into His eyes and see the depth of love there—to hear His sweet voice saying, "Don't be afraid. Everything is going to be all right. You were healed because of your faith. Go in peace." Oh, to see Him with human eyes and hear with your own ears the sound of His voice speaking peace to your heart.

Do you have any idea who He is? He is the one who created the universe—the great God almighty. He's the one who hung the stars in the heaven—who rounded the hills in the hollow of His hand. He's the one who came to earth a fragile babe, who grew to manhood teaching, healing, loving. He is the promised Savior of the world, the Rose of Sharon, the Lily of the Valley, the one who speaks peace to the raging sea—the one who speaks peace to the troubled heart.

And oh, my dear, He healed you. He called you "daughter." And I am sure (though none of the gospel writers—all men—recorded it), He called you by name—Elizabeth.

Elizabeth—Hebrew Elishaba—"The Lord is good fortune."

REFLECTING

What is the most difficult situation you have ever experienced?

Have you ever experienced despair? Can you think of some words that describe how that felt?

To whom did you turn for comfort and/or support during the time of despair?

Complete this sentence: "This time in my life is like _____."

What gives you hope?

JAIRUS' DAUGHTER

One of the synagogue rulers named Jairus, came. Seeing Jesus, he fell at his feet and pleaded earnestly with him. "My little daughter is dying. Please come and put your hands on her so that she will be healed and live." So Jesus went with him. (The woman with the issue of blood interrupts.) Some men came from the house of Jairus, the synagogue ruler. "Your daughter is dead," they said. "Why bother the teacher anymore?" Ignoring what they said, "Jesus told the synagogue ruler, "Don't be afraid; just believe." He did not let anyone follow him except Peter, James and John, the brother of James. When they came to the home of the synagogue ruler, Jesus saw a commotion, with people crying and wailing loudly. He went in and said to them, "Why all this commotion and wailing" The child is not dead but asleep." But they laughed at him. After he put them all out, he took the child's father and mother and the disciples who were with him, and went in where the child was. He took her by the hand and said to her, "Talitha, cumi" which means "Little girl, I say to you, get up!" Immediately the girl stood up and walked

around. She was twelve years old. At this they were complete-
ly astonished. He gave strict orders not to let anyone know
about this, and told them to give her something to eat.
                                                Mark 5:22–24;35–43

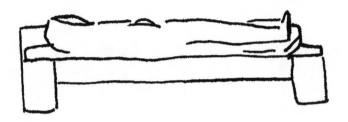

Dear Little One,

DO YOU REMEMBER ANYTHING ABOUT dying? Did you see heaven? Were you in God's presence? One thing I do know: you were always in God's care. Twelve is an interesting age—not quite a woman, but no longer a child—certainly too young to die. I think of your parents—their desperation—sitting night after night beside your bed, hoping against hope—praying for a miracle and despairing as they saw you slipping away. You were their only child. I'm sure they had great plans for you—dreams of a good marriage, grandchildren, a happy life. And now the unthinkable has happened.

I'm sure they tried everything to pull you from death's grasp—doctors, medicines, everything they could think of. I wonder who thought of Jesus from Nazareth, the Holy Man, the Healer. I wonder with what trepidation or with what hope your father set out to fetch Him.

And then there was the terrible delay. Did your father tell you later how he had engaged Jesus to come lay hands on you when there was that infernal interruption—some unclean woman Jesus stopped to heal? Don't you know your father wanted to push her out of the way and shout, "You don't have time for this! You don't understand. My child, my only child is dying. Please, please, come now!" And then the terrible news, "It's too late. She's gone." Don't you know your father must have been out of his mind with grief?

Jesus did the strangest thing: He said what the angel said to the shepherds on Bethlehem's plain: "Fear not." And then He said, "Believe—only believe. Have faith. She's going to get well." I tell you, most people would have had difficulty believing that.

When they arrived at your house, the professional mourners were already there weeping and wailing—making an awful racket. Jesus asked what they thought they were doing. "She's not dead," He said. "She's only sleeping." Of course this caused a great scornful shout of laughter at His foolishness. So He put them all out of the house. He and your mother and father and his three best friends crowded into your cramped little bedroom. And there, present in that small space, was the total creative life force of the universe and one apparently dead child. Jesus spoke two Syriac words: "*Talitha, cumi*"—"Little girl, little lamb, get up." Immediately, you put your feet on the floor and stood up and walked. That's when Jesus said, "Are you hungry, honey?" And He smiled and ordered you a snack.

He also requested that this be kept secret. But who could keep this miracle a secret? No one in the neighborhood could talk about anything else. People ran from door to door with the news. "Have you heard what the Galilean has done now?" The tidings spread like wildfire, like goose down on the wind.

Of course, your parents were astonished and deliriously happy. But it wasn't your parents' faith that healed you. They had none. Your hovering life remained because Jesus took such sweet pleasure in working this miracle of joy and grace. Joy and Grace. Those wouldn't be bad names for you, but I'm naming you Anastasia.

Anastasia - Greek "Resurrection"

REFLECTING

How have you experienced the grace of God?

What has been the happiest experience of your life?

Do you contemplate your own death?

What are the emotions you feel when you think of dying?

If you had a choice, how would you like to die?

How does faith affect the way you think about death?

THE SISTERS OF JESUS

Coming to his hometown, he began teaching the people in their synagogue, and they were amazed. "Where did this man get this wisdom and these miraculous powers?" they asked. "Isn't this the carpenter's son? Isn't his mother's name Mary and aren't his brothers James, Joseph, Simon and Judas? Aren't all his sisters with us? Where then did this man get all these things?" And they took offense at him. But Jesus said to them, "Only in his hometown and in his own house is a prophet without honor."

Matthew 13:54–57

Dear Sisters,

I DON'T EVEN KNOW HOW many of you there are. Matthew writes that people in your hometown were astonished at Jesus' teaching—His wisdom and His mighty works. They named your other four brothers: James, Joseph, Simon and Judas, and they said "all" His sisters are here. "All" indicates three or more. Otherwise they would have said, "both." You are not named, of course. Those men who wrote the gospels were such creatures of their time. Women really didn't count, except with Jesus. I'm surprised Matthew even mentioned your mother by name.

What was it like growing up in your family? Do you think your mother was partial to her firstborn? Was there any sibling rivalry—any jealousy? I assume Jesus did everything right. How is it to have a perfect brother? How old were you when you lost your dad? Did Jesus take over as parent? If so, how did you feel about that? When Jesus said, "A prophet is not without honor save in his own country," He added, "and in his own house." That makes me think there may have been some conflict in your family. It's not surprising really when you think of it. I know that your mother and brothers sought to bring Jesus home once, thinking He had somehow slid off the rails.

Did you ever really know Him? Did you ever come to believe just who Jesus is as did your brother, James, after the crucifixion? Did you recognize Him as Messiah? Did you own Him as Savior and

Lord as your mother did even before His birth? Did you ever talk to your mother about the circumstances surrounding His birth? I mean, angels, and a star, and wise men, and Herod's trying his best to kill Him before He could grow up to be king—the trip to Egypt and all the Old Testament prophecies coming true. The public records become incredibly convincing—and yet, you lived in the same house with Him year after year and knew Him only as your brother. We have no assurance that you came to belief. I think it is highly likely that it is easier for me to believe in Him twenty centuries removed than for you—though I envy your nearness to Him. You spoke with Him. You could hug Him goodnight. You could listen to Him laugh. What I wouldn't give for those experiences.

I pray you came to believe in Him. I believe that you did. How could you not, considering His kindness, tenderness, and understanding? Because of His regard for women, I imagine he showed deep respect for you and for all His sisters. A personality like His has great effect in a family setting.

I'm naming you Althea, hoping you found Him to be the way, the truth, and the life. And you, second sister, I name Alma, praying you accepted Him as Lord. And you, sister number three, I name Amanda, made worthy by His love.

Althea—Greek "truth"
Alma—Latin "soul"
Amanda—Latin "worthy of love"

REFLECTING

To whom do you presently look for support? Is that person a member of your family of origin?

Do you have a friend who is like a sister or brother?

In the family in which you grew up, who was the person who loved and nurtured you?

Who in your family has caused you pain?

Whom do you trust?

Who prays for you?

THE WOMAN TAKEN IN ADULTERY

Jesus went to the Mount of Olives. At dawn he appeared again in the temple courts where all the people gathered around him, and he sat down to teach them. The teachers of the law and the Pharisees brought in a woman caught in adultery. They made her stand before the group and said to Jesus. "Teacher, this woman was caught in the act of adultery. The Law Moses commanded us to stone such women. Now what do you say?" They were using this question as a trap in order to have a basis for accusing him. But Jesus bent down and started to write on the ground with his finger. When they kept on questioning him, he straightened up and said to them, "If any one of you is without sin, let him be the first to throw a stone at her." Again he stooped down and wrote on the ground. At this, those who heard began to go away one at a time, the older ones first, until only Jesus was left, with the woman still standing there. Jesus straightened up and asked her, "Woman, where are they? Has no one condemned you?"

"No one, sir," she said. "Then, neither do I condemn you,"
Jesus declared. "Go now and leave your life of sin."
John 8:3–11

Dear Lady,

I CAN'T THINK OF ANYTHING more humiliating than to be hauled publicly out of a bed I shouldn't be in. When I read your story, I always find great interest in the fact that you were the one dragged into the light of day to be judged. Doesn't it take two to commit adultery? So, where was the man? Adultery in Bible times is such a complicated matter. Were you married? Was he married? If you were married and he was not, the man committed adultery—the crime was against your husband. You were your husband's property. Your husband was the one defrauded. If your paramour was married and you were not, he merely committed fornication, though to be sure, he was unfaithful to his wife and that particular sin seems to have been quite popular through centuries and cultures. What was most important in all of this is that, if out of an adulterous act you became pregnant, the crime against your husband would be more serious since the big question always was that a man's child be undeniably his own. That's why virginity was so protected. If you produced a bastard child, that child must not inherit with legitimate heirs. Protecting the family name was important for the lineage and the continuation of the male line through generations.

I doubt you were thinking about all that when the scribes and Pharisees, after spying on you, grabbed you and flung you into the accusing circle. They were testing Jesus, of course. If He said you should be forgiven, they would have quoted the Law of Moses. If He said you should be stoned, they would have accused Him of cruelty toward a helpless woman. It's called "damned if you do, and damned if you don't." It was designed to catch Him in either disobeying the Law or condemning you to death. What must have you been thinking? You knew you were guilty without a shadow of an excuse. Did you expect Jesus to condemn you to death?

Imagine your surprise when Jesus didn't say a word. So much has been guessed about what He wrote in the dirt. Could it have been the multiple sins of your accusers? Whatever He wrote stopped them in their tracks. They quietly fled the scene one by one. I love that Jesus looked at you and asked, "Where are your accusers? Hasn't anyone condemned you? You must have been shaking like a leaf when you managed to answer: "No man, Lord." What relief to hear Him say, "I don't condemn you either." I think He said it gently. I think He looked at you with love. And then He added a cautionary tone as He admonished you not to sin anymore. That's a tall order. We will never know if you decided to behave in righteousness, but I have an idea that, from that day, because mercy you were given, mercy you gave.

What shall I name you? I think you must be called Mercedes.

Mercedes—Latin "Mercy"

REFLECTING

Have you ever felt unjustly judged by others?

Have you ever done something wrong and you found yourself without excuse?

Do you sometimes judge others for behavior of which you do not approve?

Why do you think in our culture sexual sins seem to be judged more harshly than other sins?

What do you think of Jesus' tendency to forgive sins of the flesh and be harder on the morally upright religious types?

What would it mean for you to look upon others as Jesus did?

What would happen to the world if everyone truly followed the example Jesus set?

THE WOMAN AT THE WELL

He had to go through Samaria. So he came to a town in Samaria called Sychar, near the plot of ground Jacob had given to his son Joseph. Jacob's well was there, and Jesus, tired as he was from the journey, sat down by the well. It was about the sixth hour. When a Samaritan woman came to draw water, Jesus said to her, "Will you give me a drink?" His disciples had gone into the town to buy food. The Samaritan woman said to him, "You are a Jew and I am a Samaritan woman. How can you ask me for a drink? For Jews do not associate with Samaritans. Jesus answered her, "If you knew the gift of God and who it is that asks you for a drink, you would have asked him and he would have given you living water." "Sir," the woman said, "You have nothing to draw with and the well is deep. Where can you get this living water? Are you greater than our father Jacob, who gave us the well and drank from it himself, as did also his sons and his flocks and herds?" Jesus answered, "Everyone who drinks of this water will be thirsty again, but whoever drinks the water I give him will never thirst. Indeed, the water I give him will become in him a spring of water welling up to eternal life." The woman said to him, "Sir, give me this water so that I won't get thirsty and have to keep coming here to draw water."... The woman said, "I know that Messiah is coming. When he comes, he will explain everything to us." Then Jesus declared, "I who speak to you am he." Then, leaving her water jar, the woman went back to the town and said to the people, "Come, see a man who told me everything I ever did. Could this be the Christ?" They came out of the town and made their way toward him.

John 4:6–29

Dear Samaritan Woman,

WELL, YOU CERTAINLY CAUSED A stir in Sychar! You turned out to be an evangelist. Imagine that! What started out to be a discussion of racial inequality ended up a lesson in theology. Everyone knew the Jews were God's chosen people—and how important racial purity had become. Jews did not want to be tainted with the kind of impurity the Samaritans lived with on a daily basis. You were certainly forthright in your objection to drawing water for this Jewish Rabbi. What was He doing in Samaria anyway? His friends had gone to buy food. Weren't they fearful of some kind of contamination from those dirty half-breeds whose country they had entered? When Jesus mentioned "living water"—the kind that would free you from drawing it out of the well and lugging it to your house—you became very interested. My grandmother carried water on the farm years ago. I tried it a time or two. If I had to do it every day, I would jump at any chance not to have to do it ever again.

When Jesus told you to call your husband, you must have must have thought, *What is this all about? What does my husband have to do with this discussion?* And you decided just to tell the truth. "I'm not married." Well, that led to an interesting discussion. "That's right," He said. "You're not married. You have been married five times and now you are living in an illicit relationship with another man who is not your husband." Did He say it sarcastically? Did you hear accusation and blame in His voice? When people of my century read this, we generally say something like, "Well, this old girl has slept around." But when we remember that women in your day could not divorce their husbands (only men could divorce their wives, and they were permitted to divorce for the most minor of infractions), we are reminded that you may have been more victim than perpetrator. The men in your life treated you shabbily, without respect, and tended to throw you out to survive the best way you could. I suppose the "best" way for you to survive was to latch on to the next man in line. I doubt this made for a healthy or happy life. Maybe you just acted out of desperation. I have observed that when things get really desperate, Jesus tends to show up.

You could see there was something special about Jesus. You admitted that He must be some sort of a prophet. You really didn't want to talk about all the men in your life, so you steered the conversation to a theological debate. Where is the true place of worship? It was a way of dodging more painful subjects. When you finally said, "I know that when Messiah comes...," Jesus answered: "You are looking at him." Did you get it? Did you fully understand that you stood in the very presence of the One promised at the beginning of creation—the One about whom God made the covenant with Abraham—the One about whom every Jewish parent had prayed through countless years, "God, let my daughter bear Messiah."

You came to believe it, didn't you? You left your water jar—not something to be treated with careless abandon. You went into the city and told everyone you encountered: "I met a man (that was nothing new), but this man knew everything about me. This man was different. This man offered me living water. I can feel it bubbling up from deep inside my heart. It feels like hope. It feels like all the love, joy, and forgiveness I always craved and never possessed. It is eternal life, this living water. Because I met Jesus at the well, I will never thirst again. My name is Hope."

Old English ... Hope

REFLECTING

How do you react to Jesus' interactions with persons of low estate?

Who in our culture would be considered by some as "lower class" or "different"?

How do you think about people who are "not like you"?

What gives you hope?

What do you understand about "living water"? Who is eligible to receive it?

PETERS'S WIFE'S MOTHER

When Jesus came into Peter's house, he saw Peter's mother-in-law lying in bed with a fever. He touched her hand and the fever left her, and she got up and began to wait on them.
Matthew 8:14–15

As soon as they left the synagogue, they went with James and John to the home of Simon and Andrew. Simon's mother-in-law was in bed with a fever, and they told Jesus about her. So he went to her, took her hand and helped her up. The fever left her and she began to wait on them.
Mark 1: 29–30

Dear Simon Peter's Mother-in-Law,

WHAT MUST YOU HAVE THOUGHT of your daughter's husband? I imagine he was considered a good catch when they were courting. He was a successful local businessman after all. He wasn't afraid of hard work—reason enough for you to believe your daughter would be well-cared for and protected. No one could accuse Peter of not being a good provider. It must have been somewhat alarming when Jesus showed up and your son-in-law—solid, practical, responsible Simon Peter ran off to follow Him. Peter just dropped the fishing nets and left them there on the beach. I'd never have thought he would do such a thing. Well, now that I think of it, he always did have an impulsive streak. What did your daughter think of this rather strangely precipitous behavior? And what must you have thought? Who would take care of the business? Who would pay the bills? I know you are just a woman and you were not to have an opinion about such matters. This was a man's problem, after all. But a problem it most certainly was.

You were living under Peter's roof, were you not? I am guessing that by then you were widowed. And you must not have had sons, so it was your son-in-law who was your support. If I am right about that, I assume you were beholden to Peter and had to be careful not to criticize him for following Jesus around the countryside instead of tending to his business. I wonder if you knew who it was that Peter was following around the Galilee? Perhaps you understood better when Jesus came to Peter's house that day when you were in bed with a fever. You must have been feeling miserable, sick and weak.

There you were, too sick to lift your head from the pillow, and that crowd came piling into the house—Peter and Andrew, James and John, Jesus, and heaven knows how many others—a large group of hungry men. Someone told Jesus how sick you were. He came to your bedside and took your hand. The fever left—just like that. And then, He lifted you up. The gospel writers add that you got up and waited on them. I can only surmise that means you hurried into the kitchen and put a meal on the table. The food you prepared was probably simple but hearty. And as the men broke bread together, I imagine there was talk of the leper and the centurion's servant healed that very day—and laughter around the table. And I imagine you joined in the festivities—feeling well and strong, full of gratitude and joy. Joy! That's a good name for you.

Joy—Old French "joie." Joy

REFLECTING

What do you believe about "women's work?"

Do you believe that in our culture women and men are assigned certain roles? How has that changed over the years?

Do you believe gender determines intelligence?

Have you ever experienced a miraculous healing of the body?

Have you experienced spiritual healing? When?

How would you characterize the dealings Jesus had with women? How was this different from the way women were perceived by others in that culture?

PETER'S WIFE

Don't we have the right to take a believing wife along with us, as do the other apostles and the Lord's brothers and Cephas (Peter)?

I Corinthians 9:5

Dear Wife of Simon Peter,

I HAVE A CONFESSION TO make. I would not even have known Simon Peter had a wife if not for the fact that he had a mother-in-law whom Jesus healed of a fever. Then, a good friend pointed out I Corinthians 9:1–5, where the Apostle Paul defended his apostleship. "Am I not an apostle? Am I not free? Have I not seen Jesus Christ, our Lord?" Then, just look at verse five: "Don't we have the right to take a believing wife along with us, as do the other apostles and the Lord's brothers and Cephas (Peter)?" Oh, my soul! There you are! And you are called "a believing wife."

So, this opens all kinds of questions. When your husband dropped his fishing nets on the beach and followed Jesus that day long ago, did you go with him? Or, did you become a believer later? Were you one of the many women who followed Jesus from Galilee—from the earliest days of His ministry? Were you one of the women who helped support Jesus and His disciples out of your own pocket?

Did you witness the feeding of the five thousand? Did you hear Him teach? Did you see Him embrace the little children? Did He teach you to pray? Did you see Him heal the lame and the blind? Were you at the cross?

During those terrible hours that led to His crucifixion, were you aware that Peter had tried desperately to disassociate himself from Jesus? Did you know that your husband denied Him—not once, but three times? Where were you when all this transpired? Later, did Peter allow you to comfort him, or was he so horrified by his own behavior that he pushed you away? Were you at the tomb? And afterwards, were you a part of the group of one hundred and twenty in the upper room? Were you present when your husband preached the sermon at Pentecost? Were you there when God's Holy Spirit fell in such power that three thousand people came to belief? Did you hear the mighty rushing wind? Did you see the flames of fire? Did you hear the many languages?

I remember revival meetings when I was a child. I remember the presence of the Holy Spirit and the conversions, and the changed lives. Those revival meetings marked my life. Those revivals were never as spectacular as the day your husband preached at Pentecost, of course, but they brought great spiritual blessing. Those times of spiritual refreshing changed people from ordinary to extraordinary—totally dedicated to Christ. I know many young people who dedicated all of life to the Lord—preachers and missionaries called out through a

"Pentecost" experience. I wish I could have seen what you saw that day—and experienced what you experienced. Oh, to have been there!

Your husband was radically changed from the person he was before. "Amazing" is the word that describes what God can do with the most unlikely of people. The day he was called, Simon Peter was promised that he would become a fisher of men. Three thousand is an impressive catch, and quite an addition to the original one hundred and twenty believers.

If you were a part of it all (and I suspect you were), you faithfully followed Jesus from Galilee all the way to the cross and into the earliest days of the church. I shall name you Fidelia.

Fidelia—Latin "Faithful"

REFLECTING

What does it mean to follow Jesus?

Which faithful Christ followers have influenced you?

Whom have you influenced for good?

How many sermons have you heard through the years? How many do you remember?

How many sermons have you seen lived out? How many of them do you remember?

MOTHERS WHO TOOK THEIR CHILDREN TO JESUS

Mothers were bringing little children to Jesus to have him touch them, but the disciples rebuked them. When Jesus saw this, he was indignant. He said to them, "Let the little children come to me, and do not hinder them, for the kingdom of God belongs to such as these. I tell you the truth, anyone who will not receive the kingdom of God like a little child will never enter it." And he took the children in his arms, put his hands on them, and blessed them.

Mark 10:13–16

Dear Moms,

WASN'T IT EXCITING? JESUS WAS going to be in your neighborhood. I can hear the chatter now. "Let's go see him." "Yes, let's go." "Did you hear that he healed that little boy? Wasn't it wonderfully amazing?" "I saw Jesus on the edge of town last time he was here. There was a huge crowd, but I was close enough to see his face. He has such a nice face—and kind eyes." "Do you suppose we could take our children?" "Oh, yes, let's take the children."

So, all you moms washed and mended the children's clothes, washed grimy little hands and faces, and set out to receive the blessing. When you saw Jesus and His friends you hesitated. They were obviously resting. Jesus had been preaching and teaching in Capernaum before He came to Judea, east of the Jordan. Wherever He went He was mobbed. Everyone wanted to hear Him. Everyone was either sick or had a sick friend or relative. They all needed healing. No wonder Jesus was tired.

As you approached, carrying infants and toddlers and holding the hands of your other little ones, you encountered several very large men blocking your way.

"What do you want?" The question was rude.

The response was gentle. "We come asking the Master to bless our children."

"Can't you see he's resting? He doesn't have time for you or your children. Go away. Go back home where you belong."

Then Jesus opened his arms, and shaking His head at His disciples, He said, "Oh, no. Don't send them away. Let the little children come to me. The Kingdom of heaven is made up of just such sweet innocence. Don't hinder them. I tell you, everyone must receive the Kingdom of God like these children do. Otherwise, they will not enter."

And then, like a Jewish father with his children every Sabbath, He took them to Himself, laid hands on them and blessed them. I'm sure you young mothers stood by and watched with great pride as He laid holy hands on each child as He looked into each sweet face with eyes full of love. Jesus always showed such tenderness and awareness of "the least of these." His healing of the sick, His loving touch, His care for the poor, His attention to the forgotten, His kindness to children mark a sharp departure from the Law. He said He didn't come to destroy the Law but to fulfill it, to fill it full of love.

This story of Jesus' blessing the children takes me back more than seventy-five years when my mother took me to visit our new pastor. I was in kindergarten at the time, and I remember thinking, *This must be Jesus*. He was big, and I was small. He had kind eyes and gentle hands. He took my face in both his hands and looked into my eyes, just like Jesus did that day so long ago. And he whispered, "God bless you, little one." I didn't understand then why my mother cried. Now, I do. Theirs is the kingdom. Ours is the kingdom. We are children of the King. I can't name all of you, but I will name the mother who spoke with the disciples. Her name is Evelyn.

Evelyn—from Eve—Hebrew "Chava"—Life

REFLECTING

Has anyone ever rained on your parade? Do you know a person who is invariably negative? How do you respond to such a person?

Has anyone ever been rude to you? How do you respond in the face of such behavior?

Why do you think Jesus said that to enter the kingdom of heaven we must become as little children?

What qualities do children possess that are precious in God's sight?

How does Jesus in his teachings go beyond the Ten Commandments?

Who has blessed you?

PILATE'S WIFE

While Pilate was sitting on the judge's seat, his wife sent him this message: "Don't have anything to do with that innocent man, for I have suffered a great deal today in a dream because of him."

Matthew 27:19

Dear Wife,

DREAMS AND PORTENTS: YOU BELIEVE in them, don't you? I suppose most people did in your day, and some still do. I think of dreams recorded in scripture: Jacob's dream of the ladder reaching from earth to heaven, Joseph's dreams of greatness that so annoyed his brothers,

Pharaoh's dream of fat and thin cattle, Solomon's dream in which God promises this son of David that he can have anything he wants. And in the New Testament, Joseph's dream: "Do not be afraid, Joseph, to take Mary for your wife. That which is conceived in her is of the Holy Spirit."

Are you the only woman in the Bible who had a dream? Your dream was disturbing. It came as a warning. It left you sleepless, alarmed, alarmed enough to warn your husband from having anything to do with Jesus, that innocent man.

You never told anyone exactly what it was you dreamed. If you could speak today, would you share your dream? It must have been vivid and unforgettable. I can almost hear you speaking:

"Something dreadful will happen. I know it. I dreamed it. Last night I dreamed that I was in a huge crowd of people. The sun was beating down on us and it was horribly hot and dusty. Everyone in the crowd was pushing and shoving. Suddenly, I looked up and saw before me a tall platform. On it was a table with a basin. Behind the table stood my husband, Pontius Pilate, Governor of Judea. He was washing his hands, but he was not washing his hands in water. He was washing his hands in blood. Suddenly, the basin tipped over, and the blood spilled out covering the table. It ran down and formed a huge pool on the platform, and then I saw a great wave of blood, like the waves on the sea, washing toward the crowd. It crashed in and covered us all. The blood covered everyone. It covered me. I felt I was drowning in it. I awoke from my dream terrified and with a sense of dread that I could not shake. I sent word to my husband and told him of my dream. I warned him to have nothing to do with the Nazarene, that innocent man. I told him that

I knew something dreadful would happen if the man was unjustly condemned. Do you know what he said to me? He said, 'Oh, my dear, you are much too emotional. Set your mind at ease. This matter does not concern you.' And when I tried to convince him, he would hear no more. Something dreadful will happen. And I am terrified."

Well, you were right. Something dreadful did happen.

You are named "Claudia Procula" in secular history, though you remain unnamed in scripture. I'll name you Alda.

Alda: Old German—Wise

REFLECTING

Do you believe God still communicates with people through dreams?

Have you ever had a dream that you felt was God's way of speaking to you?

In what ways does God have of getting your attention?

Can you think of times when God has been at work in your world?

Do you believe God knows your name?

THE WIDOW OF NAIN

Jesus went to a town called Nain, and his disciples and a large crowd went along with him. As he approached the town gate, a dead person was being carried out, the only son of his mother, and she was a widow. And a large crowd from the town was with her. When the Lord saw her, his heart went out to her and he said, "Don't cry." Then he went up and touched the coffin, and those carrying it stood still. He said, "Young man, I say to you, get up!" The dead man sat up and began to talk, and Jesus gave him back to his mother. They were all filled with awe and praised God. "A great prophet has appeared among us," they said. "God has come to help his people." This news about Jesus spread throughout Judea and the surrounding country.

Luke 7:11–17

Dear Widow of Nain,

I'M NOT SURE YOU ARE aware of what happened the day before you met Jesus, or just why such a large crowd was following Him. Jesus healed the servant of a Roman military officer in Capernaum. Word got around and large crowds of people began to follow Jesus everywhere.

The next day after that healing, Jesus, His disciples and a crowd of the curious, entered your little town of Nain. (I looked it up on a map and found that it lay eight miles south of Nazareth at the base of Mount Tabor, a day's journey from Capernaum.) As you well know, anyone who goes to Nain must climb uphill into the town by way of a narrow, rocky path. Just as Jesus and the following crowd reached the city limits, they encountered another large crowd of people coming the other way. The funeral procession approached with all the attendant fanfare, professional mourners crying out their grief, musicians playing their flutes and cymbals, and pallbearers carrying the wicker basket with the body.

Your son, your only son whom you loved devotedly had died. Not only did you love him, but also he had supported you financially since the death of your husband. He was a good son who did his duty toward his mother. Everyone in Nain agreed that though you were a widow, you were fortunate to have such a dedicated and hardworking boy.

"That boy takes good care of his mother." That's what they all said. And now you suffered this catastrophic loss. Who would have guessed that your son would have preceded you in death? That's not the way it is supposed to happen. Parents are supposed to die first.

The moment Jesus saw you, He was moved with deepest compassion. In your culture, the prevailing attitude toward compassion was that it was a weakness. Men, particularly, were not to feel emotion, and they were certainly not to express it publicly. Stoicism was valued. Emotionalism was discounted. In spite of all that, Jesus felt deep pain because of your grief. I am reminded of the prophet Isaiah when he spoke of the coming Messiah: "Surely he hath borne our griefs and carried our sorrows...." Did anybody in that crowd realize that they stood in the very presence of the promised one?

Jesus spoke to you. "Don't cry," He said. You must have been weeping with the pain of loss. And there was Jesus. He stepped over to your son and, risking the worst kind of defilement brought on by contact with the dead, Jesus touched the lifeless body and commanded that your son get up. As your child blinked, inhaled, sat up, and began talking, I can only imagine the corporate intake of breath from the crowd as they reacted, astonished witnesses to this miracle. Jesus must have been smiling as He delivered your son to you alive, healthy, exultant. Immediately, great joy replaced grief and sorrow.

The awe-filled crowd named Jesus a prophet. They sang praises, saying that God had come to help His people. And, once again, the word about Him was out. The fame of the Galilean spread throughout Judea and beyond its borders. I imagine you were more amazed than anyone. Your son was dead and was now alive again.

Because it is by the grace of God that your son was restored to you, and because of your sincere gratitude, I'll name you "Grace."

Grace: Latin "gratia" thankful, God's favor

REFLECTING

Have you suffered the loss of a loved one?

How did you grieve?

Are you a person who expresses emotions freely?

What do you think about people who choose to grieve privately?

How have you experienced God's grace?

THE WOMAN WHO ANOINTED JESUS AT SIMON'S HOUSE

Now one of the Pharisees invited Jesus to have dinner with him, so he went to the Pharisee's house and reclined at the table. When a woman who had lived a sinful life in that town learned that Jesus was eating at the Pharisee's house, she brought an alabaster jar of perfume, and as she stood behind him at his feet weeping, she began to wet his feet with her tears. Then she wiped them with her hair, kissed them and poured perfume on them. When the Pharisee who had invited him saw this, he said to himself, "If this man were a prophet, he would know who is touching him and what kind of woman she is—that she is a sinner." Jesus answered him, "Simon, I have something to tell you." "Tell me, teacher," he said. "Two men owed money to a certain moneylender. One owed him five hundred denarii, and the other fifty. Neither of them had the money to pay him back, so he canceled the debts of both. Now which of them will love him more?" Simon replied, "I suppose the one who had the bigger debt canceled." "You have judged correctly," Jesus said. Then he turned toward the woman and said to Simon, "Do you see this woman" I came into your house. You did not give me any water for my feet, but she wet my feet with her tears and wiped them with her hair. You did not give me a kiss, but this woman, from the time I entered, has not stopped kissing my feet. You did not put oil on my head, but she has poured perfume on my feet. Therefore, I tell you, her many sins have been forgiven—for she loved much. But he who has been forgiven little loves little." Then Jesus said to her, "Your sins are forgiven. The other guests began to say among themselves, "Who is this who even forgives sins?" Jesus said to the woman, "Your faith has saved you; go in peace."

Luke 7:36–50

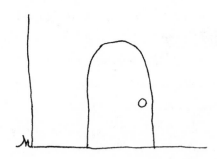

Dear Woman,

IN MY CENTURY, WE CALL it "crashing the party." Anyone who shows up to dinner uninvited will, at best, be frowned upon, and, at worst, be ejected by officers of the law. I know that it was not unusual in your time and place for anyone off the street to enter a house just to observe the well-heeled at dinner. Anyway, you didn't come to eat. You came to anoint Jesus. I don't know if you recognized

Him as Messiah, but you did know He was a holy man worthy of the gift you proffered. Where on earth did you get it—that expensive perfume? Did some inebriated customer leave it at your bedside? Did you buy it with money you earned in a profession known as the oldest? Or was it an inheritance worth more than enough to get you out of town and into a more respectable life? Was it a dowry? Wherever it came from, we know it was costly. I hate to be blunt, but I shall ask you the question: were you a prostitute? Were you, that night, repenting of a shameful past?

At Simon's house, Jesus reclined at table as was the custom. His left elbow rested on the table, His cheek in His open left palm, leaving His right hand free for taking food from the common dish. His feet extended behind Him. There you stood, weeping. This stands as one of the most poignant scenes in all of scripture, recalling David's tears for his dead child, or Joseph's when he was reunited with his brothers. Your tears were copious—enough to wash the Master's feet. And you dried them with your hair. You were well aware that decent women never loosed their hair in public. A woman's hair was her glory. To unbind it was erotic. The act was saved for the most private moments with her husband when he, with pleasure, pulled out the pins which bound it and watched it fall like black silk. Women of the street, however, advertised their availability with unbound hair. I doubt you were thinking of this as you wept and kissed the feet of the Holy One. You liberally poured perfume on Him, unmindful of onlookers.

Simon was certainly a character. What do you suppose he had in mind inviting Jesus over for dinner in the first place? He was a Pharisee—trained in the Law. His responsibility to God was to keep moral purity and rigorous adherence to justice, alive and well in the community. Simon had impeccable credentials and an earned reputation for righteousness. As he observed the scene playing out around his table, he did not see a repentant sinner weeping in contrition. Rather, he thought, *This Jesus must be a fake if he can't recognize a sinner when he sees one. If he really were a prophet, he wouldn't allow this woman to touch him—to contaminate him.* The very thought must have sent a shudder down his unyielding spine.

Jesus was on to Simon. I wonder if there was a twinkle in His eye when he said, "Simon, I have something to say to you." He told a little story about two men who owed money to a lender. One owed a little bit, the other a great deal. Since neither could repay their debts, the lender forgave them both.

The question Jesus asked was: "Which do you supposed loved the creditor more?"

Simon answered correctly: "The one who was forgiven more."

"Right," said Jesus.

Now, we discover that Simon had not been a gracious host. Jesus said, "Simon, I am your guest. I am here at your invitation. When I arrived, you did not wash my feet, nor did you give me a kiss. You did not anoint my head. You may be righteous, but you do not know the first thing about loving. You could take a lesson from this woman. She washed my feet with her tears. She lavished kisses upon my feet. She poured sweet perfume on my head. She has sinned greatly, but she also has a heart full of love. And because she loves much, her sins are forgiven."

Well, that was certainly unexpected. You must have felt light as a bird freed from a cage. I'm sure Simon was outraged to be compared unfavorably to a woman—any woman—but especially you.

Of course, the naysayers at the table muttered *sotto voce,* "Well, who does he think he is—forgiving sins. We know he can heal the sick and raise the dead, but forgiving sins. . .?" Can you believe they were so obtuse? Some things are beneath comment. I think it must have been at that moment that Jesus smiled at you and said, "Your faith has saved you, dear woman. Let your heart be at peace. And off you went, forever changed.

Who does not love a story with a villain, a hero, and a beautiful woman? But I need a little help with your story. All four of the gospel writers tell stories of a woman who anointed Jesus with expensive perfume. Matthew says it took place in Bethany at the house of Simon the Leper. He does not mention the woman's name, nor does he indicate she was a great sinner. John's account avers that it was Mary of Bethany and they were at Martha's house. Mark, like Matthew, sets the story in the house of Simon the Leper in Bethany. The woman is not named, nor is she called a great sinner, but Jesus called what she did an anointing. Luke sets the scene in the home of Simon who is not identified as a leper, but as a Pharisee. In John's account, the woman is a great sinner. Was there more than one anointing? The stories seem too much alike for that. I am sure that these varying accounts have given theologians something to talk about as long as theologians have been talking. Some have suggested that you may be that same Mary who lived a life of shame before you went to live in your sister's house—before you knew Jesus as a friend and sat at His feet as He taught you. I wish I could talk to you across the centuries. I have questions I wish I could ask you. Did you live a life of shame? Did you come to be a follower of The Way? Did you, after your conversion, go to Martha and ask her to take you in? If you are the same Mary, sister to Martha and Lazarus, you heard Jesus commend you twice—once in your sister's house when you sat at Jesus feet, and again when you anointed Him.

You sat at the feet of Jesus just as Saul "sat at the feet" of Gamaliel. You both were sitting at the feet of an esteemed rabbi, learning scripture—a practice women were not customarily accorded. And, in addition, you anointed Jesus.

You know, dear lady, anointing belongs to kings—done by, and to, men. Samuel anointed Saul as first king of Israel. Later, he anointed David to take Saul's place. You, my dear, anointed Jesus who is called King of Kings. Jesus commended you for this act, not because you anointed Him King, but because He knew what He was facing. He said it was done as preparation for His burial. Do you suppose that as He hung upon a Roman cross the memory of the fragrance of your perfume helped Him through the agony? We'll never know, but one thing is certain. You, who loved greatly, were forever changed by the One who loves most of all.

In case you are *not* Mary of Bethany, I think I should give you a name. I will call you Hannah.

Hannah—Hebrew—"God has favored me"

REFLECTING

What makes you weep?

Do you believe one sin is worse than another?

How have you sinned?

In what way has guilt informed your behavior?

What do you understand about forgiveness? Is it easy for you to forgive others?

Do you think forgiving involves forgetting?

THE SYROPHOENICIAN WOMAN

Jesus withdrew to the region of Tyre and Sidon. A Canaanite woman from that vicinity came to him, crying out, "Son of David, have mercy on me! My daughter is suffering terribly from demon-possession." Jesus did not answer a word. So his disciples came to him and urged him, "Send her away, for she keeps crying out after us." He answered, "I was sent only to the lost sheep of Israel." The woman came and knelt before him. "Lord, help me!" she said. He replied, "It is not right to take the children's bread and toss it to their dogs." "Yes, Lord," she said, "But even the dogs eat the crumbs that fall from their masters' table." Then Jesus answered, "Woman, you have great faith. Your request is granted." And her daughter was healed from that very hour.

Matthew 15:21–28

Dear Frantic Mother,

I WONDER HOW YOU KNEW about Jesus. I suppose His fame had reached even to your hometown. He had not traveled so far north before—and never outside of Israel. As far as I know, He had not had dealings with anyone but the Jews. Of course, having been ejected by His old friends in Nazareth, maybe He decided it was time He had some dealings with people other than "the chosen." I think He must have needed to escape, for a while, the neediness of the ever-present crowds and the hostility of the Jewish religious types. Tyre and Sidon seemed quieter places where only gentiles dwelt.

When you saw Jesus, you immediately began pleading for a cure for your daughter. I don't know what kind of diagnosis medical doctors in my culture would have suggested: schizophrenia, paranoia, anxiety. But two things I do know, your daughter was very ill and, because you loved her, you were persistent in seeking a cure. What made you so sure Jesus could help you? I am guessing that Jesus may have been a last resort for you. I wonder how long your daughter had been suffering—and how long had it been since you had experienced uninterrupted sleep. You are one tough lady. You never gave up.

I am somewhat amused at the reaction of the disciples. I can picture them with their hands over their ears, their eyes rolling in irritation, shouting at Jesus: "For heaven's sake, and in the name of our sanity, heal this woman's daughter.! She won't stop annoying us until you do. We can't abide her shrieking any longer. Heal her daughter and be rid of her!" When did you discover that the way to a cure for your daughter was to become such a nuisance that finally Jesus would relent and help you?

You begged Jesus to have pity on you and you called Him "Son of David." Did you realize that you had no right to address Him with that title? His answer to you sounds so harsh. He said, "I was sent only to the Jews." At that point you were on your knees before Him and addressed Him as "Lord." "Lord," you begged, "please, help me. You are my last resort. No one can do anything for my daughter, but I know You can heal her." His answer must have made your heart sink. "It's not right to throw the children's bread to the dogs." Was He calling you a dog? What kept you from getting angry? What kept you from giving up? Did you catch a teasing tone in His voice? Did you notice the word He used for "dog" was not the snarling, starving canines in the streets, but the word for a loved pet? Your response was saucy—impudent even. By that time you must have decided you could give as well as you got. "Even the dogs eat what falls from the table." Jesus must have been greatly pleased—at your wit, at your persistence, at your love for your daughter, and most of all, at your faith.

Your daughter was healed from that moment. All was well at last. You could sleep easy that night and for the nights to come. You could rest because your child was sleeping peacefully. I will call you Serena.

Serena—Latin—"tranquil, serene"

REFLECTING

Have you ever been annoyed by someone? What was your attitude toward that person?

What action, if any, did you take?

What does it mean for you to call Jesus "Lord?"

What does "lordship" imply?

With whom do you share your deepest concerns?

What seems to be the prevailing attitude in our culture toward mentally ill persons?

What part does wit, humor and laughter play in your life?

THE WOMEN WHO FOLLOWED JESUS FROM GALILEE

After this, Jesus traveled about from one town and village to another, proclaiming the good news of the kingdom of God. The twelve were with him, and also some women who had been cured of evil spirits and diseases: Mary (called Magdalene) from whom seven demons had come out; Joanna the wife of Chuza, the manager of Herod's household; Susanna; and many others. These women were helping to support them out of their own means.

Luke 8:1–3

But all those who knew him, including the women who had followed him from Galilee, stood at a distance, watching these things.

Luke 23:49

The women who had come with Jesus from Galilee followed Joseph and saw the tomb and how his body was laid in it. Then they went home and prepared spices and perfumes. But they rested on the Sabbath in obedience to the commandment.
                                                          Luke 23:50

On the first day of the week, very early in the morning, the women took the spices they had prepared and went to the tomb. They found the stone rolled away from the tomb, but when they entered, they did not find the body of the Lord Jesus. While they were wondering about this, suddenly two men in clothes that gleamed like lightning stood beside them. In their fright the women bowed down with their faces to the ground, but the men said to them, "Why do you look for the living among the dead? He is not here; he has risen! Remember how he told you while he was still with you in Galilee: 'The Son of Man must be delivered into the hands of sinful men, be crucified and on the third day be raised again.'" Then they remembered his words. When they came back from the tomb, they told all these things to the eleven and to all the others. It was Mary Magdalene, Joanna, Mary the mother of James, and the others with them who told this to the apostles. But they did not believe the women because their words seemed to them like nonsense.
                                                          Luke 24:1–11

Dear Women Followers,

IF YOU ASK ALL THE church-going Christians of my century how many disciples Jesus had, I venture to say most of them would answer: "Twelve." True, Jesus chose twelve men, and they are all named in Luke's gospel. I doubt many people would consider the women who followed him from the beginning of his ministry in Galilee as also being his disciples. Some of those women were named: Mary Magdalene, Johanna, and Susanna. They were among the women Jesus healed, but there were "many women" whose names we do not know. That would be you. You were the ones who supported the cause out of your own resources. And nothing more is recorded in scripture about you for the next three years.

As always, there are unanswered questions. What was the nature of the relationship between you and Jesus? How did you come to know Him? How did His male followers receive you? We can only guess. I imagine you women procured and prepared many meals along the way, but I would like to think that you also had opportunity to share the good news of the gospel with other women. Nothing the gospel writers record indicates that you women were present and active during the three years of His ministry. Not until the crucifixion narratives do you appear again.

In writing of the cross, John mentions three women by name: Mary, the mother of Jesus; Mary, the wife of Cleopas; and Mary Magdalene. The three other gospel writers, Matthew, Mark, and Luke mention all you women who followed Jesus from Galilee. They state that you stood "afar off" observing all that happened at Calvary. You must have been heartbroken, engulfed in intense grief, bewildered, and abandoned. The male disciples had fled in fear of their lives. You women stayed to the end. Of course, you had an advantage. You could operate without detection or suspicion. No one of any importance would have considered you traitors to the state. You were just a group of women. What harm could you do after all? You were there to the end of the horror—bereft, to be sure—but powerless and irrelevant.

All four gospel writers record that Roman soldiers gambled for His seamless robe. From whom did the money come to purchase such an expensive garment? Was it a gift of love for the Lord from you women who wanted Him to have the best? Luke tells of your bringing spices and ointments to prepare His dead body. These too, were costly. Perhaps Johanna, wife of Herod's finance minister, familiar with court life, contributed toward that purchase. These are probably details of no importance, but gratifying to know.

In Luke's account of Easter morning, Mary Magdalene, Johanna, and "many other women" arrive to find the tomb empty and an angel who asks, "Why do you seek the living among the dead? He is not here. He is risen. Remember what he told you while he was still with you in Galilee? He said that the Son of Man must suffer and die and would rise the third day." I can picture all of you gasping in astonishment, remembering how He taught you as you sat on some hillside. One of you must have exclaimed with startled recognition, "Oh, that's what he meant!" I can only imagine the emotions you felt: fear, incredulity, and then great rejoicing. "He is risen! He is alive! We must go and tell the men!"

Incredible, isn't it, that the greatest event in human history was first observed by a bunch of women who could not testify in a court of law because they were considered too emotional and, therefore, unreliable?

And when you told the men, true to form, they thought you were either making it up or were engaging in wishful thinking. "Nonsense," they said. And while you women were already believing and rejoicing, the men sat there doubting. This is proof enough that after God created Adam, He looked at the man he had created and said, "I can do better than this."

In the book of Acts, Luke wrote that the women were present in the upper room with that group of one hundred and twenty believers. You were a part of the infant church. You must have been there when Peter preached the keynote sermon at Pentecost from the book of Joel: "I will pour out my Spirit on all flesh and your sons and daughters will prophesy." The prophet Joel foretold it. "Your daughters will prophesy." I am absolutely certain that you did.

I wish I could name all of you Marvella.

Marvella—"Marvelous"

REFLECTING

If you had known Jesus as one of His followers, you could have observed Him every day. How would you describe Him?

What do you think of the way first century women were marginalized? Do you believe that women in our culture are also underrated or overlooked? Which? How?

Complete this sentence:
If I had been at the tomb with the women on that first Easter Day, I would have _____ .

What does Easter mean to you?

NOAH'S WIFE

The Lord was grieved that he had made man on the earth, and his heart was filled with pain. So the Lord said, "I will wipe mankind, whom I have created, from the face of the earth—men and animals, and creatures that move along the ground, and birds of the air—for I am grieved that I have made them." But Noah found favor in the eyes of the Lord.

Genesis 6:6–8

Dear Mrs. Noah,

SO, HOW LONG HAD YOU been married when your husband decided that God wanted him to build a boat in your backyard? Noah always was something of an odd duck. I can only imagine the humiliation you suffered with all the neighbors pointing, laughing, and making snide comments. How long had it been since rain had fallen in your neighborhood? I'm sure Noah looked like a fool sweating under the broiling sun, dragging in all that timber, sawing wood, and banging away with his hammer. The noise! Dear heaven, the noise! I hope you had something in your medicine cabinet for headache.

I understand the building of a boat wasn't the worst of it. When Noah began putting food out to attract animals, you must have had a thing or two to say to him. Every animal God ever created—not just adorable puppies and kittens but all of them—came creeping, slithering, or galloping in, every ghastly beast imaginable, alligators and lizards, goats, snakes, and warthogs. My soul—the bleating and barking, the mooing and meowing—must have been deafening. What a terrible racket! Why do you suppose Noah included cockroaches and mosquitoes? Surely that was over your objection. How in the world did Noah coax all those creatures on board? I keep thinking of the vessel as a "boat." In reality, it became a huge indoor zoo, barn, and aviary, in addition to being a hotel for your family.

When I think of the number of animals and people aboard, the space for storing provisions, the amount of food required, the lack of ventilation and sanitation, my mind boggles. When the vessel was loaded and God shut the door, the rain started to fall—a few drops at first, and then heavy, torrential rain. That's what my grandpa would call a "gully-washer" or a "frog-strangler." All those people who had jeered at Noah for building such a monstrosity changed their tune when they began to drown. You must have been horrified to hear them beating on the side of the ark, pleading to be let in

The rain came down and the floods came up. For forty days and forty nights, six weeks, nothing but water and darkness and the scent of *eau de barnyard* in the stifling air. I can only imagine the stench. Just think of all those animals eating and digesting and making an awful mess. I hope you were not the one who had cleanup duty.

Was it something of a shock when the rain stopped? The sudden silence must have been a relief. Opening the windows and seeing the sun was, I'm sure, an unimaginable blessing. And, after the waters receded, your family began life anew on the mountain. That's just the way it is, isn't it? We go through a period of darkness and despair, but as we trust God, we are given the blessing of sunlight and a new beginning. I'll name you April.

April—Latin "aprilis"—Open to the sun

REFLECTING

Can you think of a time when someone publicly humiliated you?

What was your response?

Have you ever been exasperated toward a loved one? What tends to irritate you?

What is the darkest passage in your story?

How would you define:
- Redemption
- Choice
- Contentment

What do you believe about second chances?

JOB'S WIFE

So Satan went out from the presence of the Lord and afflicted Job with painful sores from the soles of his feet to the top of his head. Then Job took a piece of broken pottery and scraped himself with it as he sat among the ashes. His wife said to him, "Are you still holding on to your integrity? Curse God and die!" He replied, "You are talking like a foolish woman. Shall we accept good from God, and not trouble?" In all this, Job did not sin in what he said.

Job 2:7–10

Dear Mrs. Job,

WHEN I THINK OF YOU, my heart hurts. No one seems to remember that all the terrible things that happened to your husband also happened to you. I can only imagine the extent of the devastation that befell your family. The loss of your flocks and herds and crops was bad enough, but, after all, that was only a series of economic misfortunes. The thought of the loss of your children tears at my heart and, unbidden, sends an alarm through me that stops my breath. If such tragedy can happen to you, it can happen to me. And it has happened to people I know. To lose one child is pain beyond my ability to comprehend, but to lose them all—how unutterably tragic.

I know your husband was a believer in the one true God, but I imagine you were probably disgusted with the whole thing. To you, Job must have looked foolish worshiping a God so weak he couldn't even keep your children alive. I can't imagine what you thought when you looked out and saw your husband sitting on an ash heap with those weeping sores on his body. I have to ask if you were the one who had changed the bandages all those days and nights? No wonder you were angry. You were crazy with grief and suddenly left, not only childless but without much of an idea where your next meal was coming from. And there was Job, no help at all, being true to his God. You must have been experiencing some kind of blind rage when you screamed at him to curse God and die. I can't believe Job's answer to you. I found it curt and uncaring. I understand that marriage in your culture was very different from marriage in my time and place. I know there was nothing as frivolous as "romance" when you lived, but would it not have helped if Job could have taken you in his arms to give you comfort? I wish the two of you could have wept together. I wish he could have explained to you his commitment to his God.

Job said, "Though he slay me, yet will I trust him," and, "I know that my Redeemer lives." Those words have given hope to millions of people through the long, long years. I wish Job could have shared his faith with you. Again, I know that your marriage had not much to do with love.

It was more for producing children—particularly male children. That was of great importance. But now, your whole purpose for living was destroyed along with your offspring. As long as you had them, you were the respected wife. Now, your identity was gone and I feel great sadness that your husband could not grieve with you.

It is lovely to know that Job was vindicated finally, but where were you? I doubt you were the one to bear him ten more children. Did he find a new, young wife? And even if you were able to give him a second family, you still have many graves to visit in the Uz Municipal Cemetery. No new child, however wonderful, could ever replace those first dear, lost children. Job may have been blessed more at the end than the beginning, but my breath is like a dagger when I think of your multiplied pain. And so, dear suffering wife and mother, who knew poverty, lingering affliction, and death piled on vicious death, I will name you Dolores.

Dolores—Latin "dolere" pain and sorrow

REFLECTING

Why does God allow human suffering?

In your opinion, is there any good that comes from suffering and loss?

What is the most important thing we can do for someone in deep grief?

Most people want to say something comforting to a grieving person. Here are some things that well-meaning people say:

- He's in a better place.
- God needed her more than you did.
- It was God's will.
- Heaven is sweeter because she is there.

What might be more helpful?

If you have experienced loss, what comforted you?

NAAMAN'S WIFE'S LITTLE MAID

Now Naaman was commander of the army of the king of Syria. He was a great man in the sight of his master and highly regarded, because through him the Lord had given victory to Syria. He was a valiant soldier, but he had leprosy. Now bands from Syria had gone out and had taken captive a young girl from Israel, and she served Naaman's wife. She said to her mistress, "If only my master would see the prophet who is in Samaria! He would cure him of his leprosy."

II Kings 5:1–3

When Elisha, the man of God, heard that the king of Israel had torn his robes, he sent him this message: "Why have you torn your robes? Have the man come to me and he will know that there is a prophet in Israel."

II Kings 5:8

Dear Little Maid,

I WONDER ABOUT YOU. HOW old were you when the Syrian army carried you from your home, a captive? Obviously, you were old enough to understand that Israel had a distinctive relationship to the one God. No doubt you knew stories of Abraham and Isaac, of slavery in Egypt, of plagues and blood on the doorposts. You knew of God's place in the life of Israel. And you knew of the prophet Elisha. I have an idea that you were a beautiful child—dark eyes full of light and life, a sturdy little body, and an attitude to match. When the Syrian army came to your town, I think you might have tried to hide your younger siblings. Scripture does not record information about your family. You must have shown courage and initiative to have landed on your feet in Naaman's possession. The captain of the army of Syria does not take just any ragamuffin into his home to serve his wife. When you met her, I can almost hear the conversation:

NAAMAN: "Hi, honey. I'm home."
WIFE: "Thank all the gods for your safe return."
NAAMAN: "I brought you a present." (He presents you to her.)
WIFE: "Well, now. What have we here?"
NAAMAN: "I chose the best of the lot just for you."

WIFE: "Thank you, dear. We'll get her cleaned up. I'll train her
             as my personal maid. She will be in charge of my clothes
             and cosmetics. I'll teach her to attend to my coiffeur. I
             hope she's better than the last slave you brought me. We'll
             see how she works out. You are sweet, dear, to remember
             your wife with lovely gifts. You are my good man."

NAAMAN: "Harrumph."

You observed and learned. I imagine you pleased your mistress.
Before long, you realized that in spite of the fame of your master—
in spite of his courage and high esteem he had earned—there was
something very wrong. You watched your mistress who was often in
distress. At times she wept and her eyes were always sad. You overheard
muffled conversations, and one day, another servant spoke the awful
truth: leprosy! Naaman was a leper! You were struck to the heart with
fear for him.

I can only imagine the courage it took for you to speak to your
mistress about her husband's illness. You probably approached her with
some hesitation. She might have sent you away, but when you spoke of
a cure, she listened. Your faith in the prophet Elisha was a reflection of
your faith in God. You stated with conviction: "There is a prophet in
Samaria who has the power to heal your husband."

That started a chain reaction: your mistress told Naaman. Naaman
told his boss—the king of Syria. The king of Syria sent Naaman to the
king of Israel. The king of Israel tore his robes and said, "Who does
he think I am? I'm not God. I can't cure him." Elisha heard about his
king's reaction and he THUNDERED: "WHY HAVE YOU TORN
YOUR ROBES? SEND THE MAN TO ME SO THAT HE WILL
KNOW THERE IS A PROPHET IN ISRAEL!"

Later, you learned the rest of the story. Elisha told him to dip seven
times in the Jordan. Like a spoiled child, Naaman pitched a fit and said
if that was all there was to it, Syria had better rivers than the Jordan.
Finally, he did what Elisha recommended—no—ordered—in the first

place, and Naaman was healed. The King James Version says, "His flesh was like unto the flesh of a little child." Naaman's cure was amazing enough, but more amazing was his announcement: "Now I know there is no God in all the world except in Israel." That is a ringing declaration of faith if ever there was one.

If not for you, little maid, it might never have happened. If you hadn't been captured, if you hadn't been taken to Naaman's house, if you hadn't spoken up—Naaman might not have been healed. I think of Joseph and his reunion with his brothers. He said, "You intended harm, but God meant it for good." No one, for one moment, would think it a good thing that you were yanked from your home and family and carried away into captivity. But God can, and does, bring good from evil. You were put in Naaman's house for a purpose—to bring about healing—healing of the body and healing of the spirit.

I'll name you Eudora Paige.

Eudora—Greek "Good gift"
Paige—Greek "child, young servant"

REFLECTING

There is more than one way to be held captive. Can you think of anything that holds you captive? (Think: material things, busyness, grudges, jealousy)

What kind of healing have you experienced?

How can something evil be turned into a blessing?

Have you had such an experience?

THE DAUGHTER OF JEPHTHA

And Jephtha made a vow to the Lord: "If you give me the Ammonites into my hands, whatever comes out of the door of my house to meet me when I return in triumph. . .will be the Lord's, and I will sacrifice it as a burnt offering." ... Then Jephtha went over to fight the Ammonites, and the Lord gave them into his hands.... When Jephtha returned to his home in Mizpah, who should come out to meet him but his daughter, dancing to the sound of tambourines! She was an only child.

Judges 11:30–35

You do not delight in sacrifice, or I would bring it; you do not take pleasure in burnt offerings. The sacrifices of God are a broken spirit; a broken and contrite heart. O God, you will not despise.

Psalm 51:16–17

Well, My Dear,

YOU CAME FROM UNCERTAIN PARENTAGE—NOT your fault, of course. Who was it that decreed that the sins of the fathers would be visited on succeeding generations? Your father was the child of a prostitute and an unknown father. He certainly suffered as a result—thrown out by his legitimate siblings and only welcomed back when they desperately needed him to go to battle for them. So desperate were they that they promised him great authority. He did become the ninth judge in Israel.

I doubt you were aware of the heavy negotiations that transpired between your father and his "brothers," much less the terrible vow that ended in such tragedy. Scripture records that "the Spirit of God" came upon Jephtha before he went to fight against the Ammonites. That should have given him all the courage he needed before going into battle. Instead, your father played quid pro quo with God. "If you give me victory in battle, then I'll offer in holocaust the first thing that comes out of my house to meet me when I get home." What in the name of all that's sane was he thinking? Did he imagine a servant would come out—or a pet dog or cat? Perhaps he thought his wife might make an appearance. Surely not his only child!

Well, he slaughtered the Ammonites. The victory belonged to God, after all. And your father came home. Good news travels almost as fast as bad news does. You must have heard of the victory, so you dressed in your party clothes, grabbed your tambourine, and danced out the front door to welcome your father, the conquering hero. Your father's response was probably fairly typical of him: "Daughter, look what you have done to me." This can be translated: "It's not my fault. You are the one who (fill in the blank)." And then he explained: "I have vowed a vow and I cannot undo it."

Actually, he could have. He might have gone to the Lord and said something like, "Look, Lord, it was a stupid vow to begin with. I should have trusted you because your Spirit was upon me. Instead, I made this unnecessary deal. You and I already had an agreement. Look, my child does not deserve to die because of my lack of courage. I tell you what I will do: I will give you everything I have of any material value. I will become the most honorable judge Israel has ever known. For the rest of my life I will be your man. Okay, Lord, I am trusting you to let me off the hook."

Could he not have prayed David's prayer: "For thou desirest not sacrifice; else would I give it: thou delightest not in burnt offering. The sacrifices of God are a broken spirit; a broken and a contrite heart. O God, thou wilt not despise."

But he did not. He did not understand. Before the horror of your death, he granted your wish that you and your friends would grieve together for two months at a retreat center in the mountains. You and your friends wept for all you would not experience on this earth—a life cut short. You returned to your fate. With courage you faced your father who raised the knife and plunged it into your heart. What a horrific death—a young girl sacrificed on the altar of stupidity. If is it any comfort, you are not forgotten. It is recorded that every year for four days, the daughters of Israel went together to the mountain to remember you. Their love stands as your memorial. I will name you Kara.

Kara—Latin "Caro" Dear

REFLECTING

Have you ever been the victim of someone else's thoughtlessness?

What do you think it means that the sins of the fathers are visited on their children?

How do you react to violence?

Have you discovered life is not fair? What comes to mind?

Is it important to you that after your death you will not be forgotten?

How do you want to be remembered?

POTIPHAR'S WIFE

Now Joseph was well-built and handsome, and after a while his master's wife took notice of Joseph and said, "Come to bed with me!" But he refused. "With me in charge," he told her, "my master does not concern himself with anything in the house; everything he owns he has entrusted to my care. No one is greater in this house than I am. My master has withheld nothing from me except you, because you are his wife. How then could I do such a wicked thing and sin against God?" And though she spoke to Joseph day after day, he refused to go to bed with her or even be with her. One day he went into the house to attend to his duties, and none of the household servants was inside. She caught him by his cloak and said, "Come to bed with me!" But he left his cloak in her hand and ran out of the house."

Genesis 39:6b–12

Lady Potiphar,

YOU MADE IT ABUNDANTLY CLEAR to Joseph just what you were thinking. There was nothing shy and retiring about you. You had a "see, want, get" mentality based on the idea of "I can have anything or anyone I want." So, Joseph was handsome, wasn't he? And he was "well-built"? Did you look at him and compare him to your husband? I wonder if Potiphar were beginning to sag a bit around the middle. Was he turning gray? Nodding off during conversations? Beginning to take naps in the afternoon? Perhaps, all he wanted to do in bed was sleep. Potiphar was a busy man, a great success as the world measures success. Was he so busy that he didn't pay any attention to you? Did you feel neglected? Were you angry at your husband? He had given you every material thing any woman could want. It obviously wasn't enough. Maybe, in your eyes, Potiphar was not the man he used to be. For that matter, I wonder if you were worried that you were no longer the sweet young thing who had once attracted a wealthy husband and now you had something to prove. Had you looked in a mirror and seen the first fine lines around your mouth? Had you begun plucking gray hairs from around your temples? Did you notice that your body was beginning to droop and sag? Did you worry that in a few years you would no longer be able to attract men? Had your identity always come from your knowing that you could have any man you wanted?

You may have been just another spoiled rich woman who was bored and wanted some excitement. Without a doubt, you knew how to stir things up. Your one virtue may have been your persistence. You certainly kept hammering away at poor Joseph, ordering him to do your bidding every time you could manage to be in the same vicinity with him. He—being a man of sterling integrity, excellent character, a true man of God—refused you at every turn. Being spurned may have been a new experience for you. And it must have been humiliating. Women through the centuries have sought revenge by crying, "Rape!" When Joseph fled, leaving his cloak in your hand, you may have been seeking revenge, but, more likely, you simply needed to cover your own misdeeds.

Joseph was a slave, a handsome one to be sure, but a slave nevertheless. Why did you feel it necessary to put him in such an untenable position, trusted by your husband and tempted by you? When it came to your word against his, he did not have a chance. After all, your husband preferred to believe in your fidelity to him. A slave, even a very talented one, was expendable. You, Lady Potiphar, are suffering from a deep need to control. Women in your culture, even very rich women, had practically no real power. Oh, they could boss the servants around and put fear into their inferiors. That was why it was so infuriating to you that Joseph did not immediately drop his skivvies (and his convictions) and hop into bed with you. You were not accustomed to being defied. You were able to lie about him to the other servants and to your trusting husband. Your only power and control came through manipulation and mendacity. What on earth can I possibly name you? I suppose it has to be "Lulu"—as in "Look out, boys, Lulu's back in town." Lulu—American slang—"a remarkable person

REFLECTING

How do you feel about getting older?

How much power and control do you have over other people?

What gives a person power?

How do you use the power you have?

How important is sexuality in our culture? How is it misused?

How would you describe a person of integrity?

Do you know a person who is manipulative? How have you related to that person?

SAMSON'S MOTHER

A certain man ... named Mannoah, had a wife who was sterile and remained childless. The angel of the Lord appeared to her and said, "You are sterile and childless, but you are going to conceive and have a son. Now see to it that you drink no wine or other fermented drink and that you do not eat anything unclean, because you will conceive and give birth to a son. No razor may . . . be used on his head, because the boy is to be a Nazirite, set apart to God from birth. . ."

Judges 13:2–5

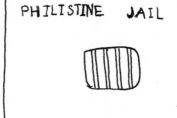

Dear Mrs. Manoah,

YOU MAY NOT KNOW THE word "theophany," but it is used by theologians when they are referring to events in the Bible when people were visited by some form of the deity. Instantly, I can think of several: Abraham and his wife, Sarah, who bore Isaac; Hagar, mother of Ishmael; Zacharias, whose wife, Elizabeth, bore John the Baptist; and Mary, of course, mother of Jesus. You were one of those women. Often, the divine message was sent to a woman who had not been able to conceive. That was true in your case. I assume you suffered the shame associated in your culture with childlessness. Scripture does not indicate, as with Sarah, that you were beyond your childbearing years, but the message came with explicit instructions for your prenatal regimen: no strong drink and no unclean food. Your child was to be a Nazirite, set apart for God.

Your association with the angel of the Lord ended with fireworks at the altar and a disappearing act that knocked you and your husband flat on the ground, making believers of you. Manoah was concerned that, having seen God, you both would die, but you, being the calm and logical person in the family, gave him good reasons not to fear.

Sure enough, nine months after the ascension of the angel, you delivered a bouncing baby boy. Scripture records that you named him. I'm glad that detail is included because naming is such a power and in your culture, usually the father's role. The fact that you named your child is particularly interesting since your own name was never mentioned. You called your son "Samson." It means "like the sun." Were you thinking of the light he would bring? Did you hope that since he was set apart unto the Lord even before his birth, he would grow up to be a life giver? What dreams we have for our children, and especially this child, announced by God's own angel. Your son was to be a Nazirite, wholly belonging to God.

Well, our dreams don't always come true. What we expect and what ultimately transpires may be two different things. Samson grew up, and he grew up strong. In spite of his wonderful, dedicated, God-fearing parents, he became involved with too many wicked women. The first time he fell in love, it was with a Philistine woman he immediately wanted to marry. He came to you and asked if you and Menoah would arrange the wedding. Your first reaction was so typical of parents from the beginning of time: "Can you not find a nice girl closer to home (and with beliefs closer to ours)?" His desire to marry a Philistine did not bode well.

I do not know how much Samson hid from you: his womanizing, the extent of his great physical strength, and heaven knows what else. Did you ever find out that he had killed a lion with his bare hands? Did you know he visited a prostitute in Gaza and afterwards carried the city gates away on his shoulders? He did a good job of compromising his relationship with God, but the Spirit of the Lord was upon him nonetheless. Strange, is it not, how God works?

Of course, Samson's meeting with Delilah can only be described as disastrous. He was such a fool when it came to her manipulative pleading. You would think he would have caught on, after two betrayals at her hands, that she was a *femme fatal.* Samson never did become the man you dreamed that he would be, a heartbreak to any mother.

I hope you were spared his death. Betrayed and blind, he called on God for superhuman strength one more time, and once more, God granted his request. Samson did not die alone. He took three thousand Philistines with him. Dying, he literally brought down the house. One more interesting detail is recorded: his brothers recovered Samson's body for burial. So, you had more children. I hope they brought you joy and contentment.

Although Samson was judge in Israel for twenty years, he did no great thing. And yet, centuries later, he is mentioned by the writer of Hebrews in the list of heroes of the faith. Perhaps God wanted him to have a decent memorial, after all.

I'll name you Salome, with the hope that God granted you some peace of heart and mind in spite of your dashed hopes and all the dreams that did not come true.

Salome—Hebrew "Shalom"—peace

REFLECTING

What have been your greatest expectations in life?

What have been your greatest disappointments?

Have you been in a situation where you desperately wanted something for someone and it did not materialize?

Have you thought you knew what was "best" for someone?

Have you found it difficult not to try to manage someone else's life?

What brings you true peace of heart and mind?

THE SHUNEMMITE WOMAN

One day Elisiha went to Shunem. And a well-to-do woman was there, who urged him to stay for a meal. So whenever he came by, he stopped there to eat. She said to her husband, "I know that this man who often comes our way is a holy man of God. Let's make a small room on the roof and put in it a bed and a table, a chair and a lamp for him. Then he can stay there whenever he comes to us."

II Kings 4:8–10

Dear Kind Lady,

I SUPPOSE THERE HAVE ALWAYS been women who cannot bear to see a man go hungry. Elisha often passed through your neighborhood. The first time you offered him something to eat, I can almost hear him saying something like, "No, really, I can't think of imposing on you." You, however, insisted. He ate that day, and it became something of a habit. Every time he passed through Shunem, he made a point to stop by your house. You were always ready for him. I'm sure the fragrance of baking bread guided Elisha straight to your kitchen table. Elisha was not the only one you fed. He always traveled with his servant, Gehazi, so you fed them both.

Do you remember the day you talked to your husband about sprucing up a spare room for the prophet? By that time, you recognized Elisha as a holy man. How kind of you and your husband to arrange accommodations for him in your home. Even God's prophets need a place to sleep. How thoughtful of you to provide a quiet place of respite. I'm sure Elisha was happy to have a private place for study and prayer.

Did you ever in your life expect Elisha to pay you? You provided for him out of a good and generous heart. You may have been surprised when he said, "Dear lady, you have lavished care on me and my servant. Is there anything I can do for you in return? Would you like for me to put in a good word for you with the king or the general of the army?" I can imagine your being flustered and saying something like: "Oh, my goodness, no. That won't be necessary. I can't think of taking payment from you." Later, Elisha asked Gehazi, "What do you think would really please this dear woman? What might we do to repay her kindness?" Gehazi pointed out that you didn't have a child. "A son would please her," he said.

When Elisha announced to you, "You will have a boy by this time next year," your response came out of years of doubting it would ever happen: "You are a man of God. You would not lie to me, would you?" And then your son was born, just as Elisha said. You might have thought about making Elisha's spare room into a nursery, but you managed to find space for the baby elsewhere. You kept Elisha's room for him just as it was.

What a delight to watch your own child grow and learn. Those first words and first steps are dear. Think of the care, love, and joy over the years. A mother's work is a constant labor of love. She is repaid in a million little ways: a gurgling laugh, a dandelion laid at her feet by grimy little hands, a sleepy head upon her shoulder, little arms that cling in sweet embrace. Too soon childhood is a thing of the past. Where do the years go? How swiftly they fly!

Your child grew to young manhood. I know that dark day of his death is seared into your brain. He complained to his father of a terrible headache that morning. The farm workers carried him into the house. You held him and rubbed his head for hours. Just at noon, he died.

The only thing you knew to do was to put your child's body on the bed of the prophet, shut the bedroom door, and hurry to Mount Carmel where Elisha was staying. You knew where to go for help. Anguish and fear propelled you to prostrate yourself, grab his feet and say, "Did I ask you for a son? No! And did I tell you not to lie to me?"

Elisha came back with you to your house, the house he knew so well. He paced the floor and prayed to God for a miracle. Then, he stretched himself over the body of your son. After what must have seemed an eternity, he called to you and gave your boy back to you.

I will call you Joanna because it was Elisha's God who gave the child to you, not once, but twice. The first time, it was at his birth after years of hopeless yearning. The second time, it was an answer to prayer, a miracle of God, almost like a second birth.

Joanna—feminine of John—Hebrew "The Lord is gracious"

REFLECTING

Do you believe that kindness is always returned?

Can you recall a time when someone showed you kindness?

What do you understand about "paying it forward?"

Do you believe in miracles?

LOT'S WIFE

But Lot's wife looked back, and she became a pillar of salt.
Genesis 19:26ff

Dear One,

IWONDER WHAT YOUR LIFE must have been with Lot as a husband. His Uncle Abraham did his best to help along the way, but Lot always managed to finagle his way out of a bad situation to his own advantage. What was he thinking when he took you and the children to live in Sodom, of all the filthy places on the earth? The little scene that played out when God decided to destroy the city is a case in point. Uncle Abe had tried to persuade God not to annihilate the place. He bargained with God over the number of righteous in the city, and finally, the Lord agreed not to destroy Sodom if only ten righteous men could be found there. Good luck with that.

Well, back to the scene. It was evening. Two angels came to the city gate. Lot went out to meet them and invite them to your home. After supper, it was time to go to bed. That was when the entire populace of the town arrived at your house banging on the door, demanding Lot throw out the two men so the whole town could engage in unspeakable behavior with them. Lot's "solution" to the situation was to suggest the two men were off limits, being guests in the house; however, he said, "I have two virgin daughters you might care to rape instead." Dear old Dad! He was always ready with a solution to any problem. While he was offering your daughters to the populace, I trust you were shielding them and shouting at him, "Over my dead body!"

As it happened, the angel-men took charge, overpowered the mob, struck the ringleaders blind, and began to ask sensible questions: "Is there anyone else in your family we need to rescue?" They gave needed information: "The Lord has sent us to destroy Sodom because of its wickedness." Lot went to warn your sons-in-law who scornfully dismissed the very idea.

As morning dawned, the angels told Lot to hurry. Lot continued to dilly-dally. What was he doing that was so all fired important? Finally, the angels grabbed your hand and the hands of your daughters and literally pulled you out of the house, down the streets, and out of the city. Just outside the city gate, one of them yelled: "Run for your life. Don't look back. Stay away from the plains. Run to the mountains!" Lot, of course, had to offer an alternative plan. "I can't escape to the mountains. I might die there," he said. "I'm going to run to the little town of Zoar." And that's where you went. At the moment you entered Zoar, God rained down fire and brimstone, totally destroying Sodom,

Gomorrah, and all the little towns on the plains. At that instant, you looked back.

Someone has suggested that you looked back because you were remembering all the pleasures of Sodom. I do not believe that for one moment. I think you looked back because your married daughters were in that city. Their husbands, your sons-in-law, refused to listen to reason and their disbelief cost all of them their lives. How distressing!

You would be further distressed if you knew that after you were out of the picture, your two virgin daughters, the ones your husband offered to the mob, decided they should "preserve their father's seed." Two nights in a row they got him so drunk that he did not know what he was doing. Both girls turned up pregnant. The two boys born of this abomination could truthfully say, "My daddy was also my grandpa." Can you beat that! By the way, I'm naming you Sally.

Sally—Latin … "sal"—salt

REFLECTING

How would you define "sin?"

Explain the difference between sinning against God and sinning against another person.

Do you believe "what goes around comes around?"

Do you believe sin always has consequences?

What do you believe about grace?

MOTHER OF JABEZ

Jabez was more honorable than his brothers. His mother had named him Jabez, saying, "I gave birth to him in pain." Jabez cried out to the God of Israel, "Oh, that you would bless me and enlarge my territory! Let your hand be with me, and keep me from harm (KJV version says, "evil") so that I will be free from pain." And God granted his request.

I Chronicles 4:9–10

Dear Mom,

YOU BARELY RECEIVED HONORABLE MENTION by the writer of the book of Chronicles. Your boy's name came up in an obscure couple of verses tucked in the middle of a long list of names, a genealogy of the family of Judah. Those verses mentioned your sons without saying how many of them you had. The account in scripture only tells us that your sons were dishonorable, which makes me wonder what sins they had committed. Which of the commandments had they broken? What sort of reputation did they have in your town? Obviously, they were the cause of great shame for you—nothing to brag about.

You named your new child "Jabez." It means "causing pain." The NIV says you named him that because you gave birth to him "in pain." The KJV states you bore him "with sorrow." Those are two very different things. Every woman who has opted for natural childbirth can attest to the fact that birthing a baby causes physical pain no matter how often the attending physician says, "You may feel some discomfort," or refers to labor pains as "contractions." Any woman who has ever borne a child the size of a bowling ball can tell you that birthing a baby hurts.

Sorrowing is quite another matter. I'm wondering if you were simply worn out with grief over your older boys. They had not turned out as you had hoped and planned. They might have been darling little children who brought you great joy until they hit puberty and then went wild. Adolescence is a difficult phase for some people. Perhaps if they had had a strong father figure, or an active youth group with positive role models, things would have been different. When you were pregnant again, you may have been too tired to cope with another disappointment. And since you had older children, I have to ask if Jabez was a change of life baby? Did he come as a surprise to you when you thought you could safely sell the baby bed?

When did you discover Jabez was not like the others? He was a good boy. He observed his brothers and decided he did not want to turn out like they did. He, most likely, noticed that they had wounded you by their attitudes and behavior. He decided early to honor you by walking the straight and narrow way. Finally, you had a son of worth.

Did you know of his prayer? It has four parts. The first two parts sound a lot like prosperity theology: "Bless ME"; "Enlarge MY territory." I hear overtones of TV ministers telling their viewers, "God wants to prosper you and bless you real good, and will do it if you send me money." The second two points of your son's prayer seem more theologically sound: "I want your hand to guide me"; and "Keep me from evil." Jabez had seen sufficient evil throughout his life by watching his older brothers. He chose to avoid the lifestyle of his siblings and all the attendant unpleasant consequences. Good for him. Part of being mature is being able to make good choices. And God heard his prayer and granted his request.

You might be interested to know that many, many centuries after Jabez lived, a man named Bruce Wilkinson snatched your son from the obscurity of the genealogical list in Chronicles. He wrote a book about him entitled *The Prayer of Jabez*. You will not understand when I tell you that the book was on the *New York Times* best seller list and sold millions of copies. That book became the subject of Bible studies and conversations among people called Christians.

Publishers adapted the book for preschoolers, children, and teenagers. Many commercial items accompanied the book's popularity. "Prayer of Jabez" coffee mugs, bracelets, necklaces and sweatshirts inscribed with the prayer created an additional market. Everyone was aware of "The Prayer of Jabez." I'm sure it was a blessing to many. But, as you might have guessed, some people misused the prayer. They began repeating it as a mantra, a formula for getting God's attention, claiming that if a person repeated the prayer word for word every day for two weeks, that person's life would be changed for the better—absolutely guaranteed. I suppose that could be so, but I believe the prayer your son prayed was not so much focused on himself. I believe the prayer was focused on the God in whom Jabez believed, the God who cares and provides for His children. I know you had a good boy. Of greater significance, we have a good God.

I will name you Consuela.

Consuela—Latin *Consolar*—"Consolation"

REFLECTING

Is it wrong to pray for blessings?

Compare and contrast the Prayer of Jabez and Solomon's request for wisdom.

Can you think of a time in your life when you made a decision that was not wise? What were the consequences of that decision?

Many people believe God takes pleasure in giving His children material blessings. How do you react to that belief? How does it fit with the emphasis Jesus put on the last, the lost, and the least?

When you are in a difficult situation, where do you find consolation?

PHARAOH'S DAUGHTER

And the daughter of Pharaoh came down to wash herself at the river; and her maidens walked along by the river's side; and when she saw the ark among the flags, she sent her maid to fetch it. And when she had opened it, she saw the child: and, behold the babe wept. And she had compassion on him, and said, "This is one of the Hebrews' children."

Exodus 2:5–6

Dear Daughter of Pharaoh,

YOU HAD NO IDEA WHAT you started. Rarely does a person who has nothing more in mind than to take a bath inadvertently influence the history of two nations. When you opened that little ark and took one look at the red-faced, screaming baby, you could not resist him. Your compassion was instantaneous. Immediately, you knew it was one of the doomed Hebrew infants, condemned to death by your father. Everything in you told you to close that ark, turn your back, and walk (or wade) away. It was none of your business. I wonder, though, if you disagreed with your father. Did you pity the poor condemned children and their families? And this baby, here within your power to save, was so sweet, even if he was making a big noise for such a tiny child. I suppose your motherly instincts kicked in. At that extremely weak moment for you, a little girl appeared asking if you needed a woman to nurse the baby. Was this a setup or what? You agreed. The little girl turned out to be the baby's older sister, Miriam. She called her mother, Jochabed, to breastfeed him. Then Jochabed took her own child back home, and you paid her for her services, a happy arrangement all the way around. The baby got fed, the birth mother had her child back (with wages for caring for him), and you had hope that, one day soon, you would have a little boy, a son, to love and spoil.

I wonder how old the child was when a heartbroken Jochabed brought him to you at the palace. She always knew the day would come when she would have to give him up. It reminds me of the day Hannah took Samuel to live with Eli in the temple, or any mother putting her six-year-old on the bus the first day of school, or any dad walking his daughter down the aisle toward a life with her new husband. So, Jochabed brought the boy to you, and he became yours. You named him—you whose name is not recorded. "Moses," you said, "because I drew him out of the water."

Because you took Moses as your son, this child of Hebrew slaves grew up in the palace with every privilege at your command: royal accommodations, fine clothes, good food, and the best education Egypt could offer. You had no idea what God was preparing for this child (and more than two million Hebrew slaves). The pharaoh, your father, was defeated, his armies destroyed, Egypt humiliated. The day you decided to save the life of a Hebrew baby, you could not possibly have foreseen the devastating consequences for your father and for your nation.

Tell me, O daughter of Pharaoh, did your father ever upbraid you over the matter? Did he shout at you that you never should have brought the Hebrew child into the palace? And, tell me, O second mother of Moses, if you had known then what you know now, would you still have taken him as your son? I shall name you Sarah. It's from the Hebrew and means "princess."

REFLECTING

What do you know about hindsight?

Have you experienced in your life the trauma of radical change?

What do you understand about being enslaved?

Do you believe that God has worked in your life?

Do you look back and see that decisions you made long ago have had consequences?

THE WIDOW OF ZAREPHATH

The word of the Lord came to him: "Go at once to Zarephath of Sidon and stay there. I have commanded a widow in that place to supply you with food." So he went to Zarephath. When he came to the town gate, a widow was there gathering sticks. He called to her and asked, "Would you bring me a little water in a jar so I may have a drink?" As she was going to get it, he called, "And bring me, please, a piece of bread." "As surely as the Lord your God lives," she replied. "I don't have any bread— only a handful of flour in a jar and a little oil in a jug. I am gathering a few sticks to take home and make a meal for myself and my son that we may eat it—and die." Elijah said to her, "Don't be afraid. Go home and do as you have said. But first make a small cake of bread for me from what you have and bring it to me...."

I Kings 17:8–13

Dear Widow of Zarephath,

WE HAVE ONLY A LITTLE information about you. You had been married. Your husband was deceased. You were a single mom, the sole support of your child. You lived in poverty. Oh, and one more thing: God spoke to you. I have to wonder exactly what God said. We know that God told Elijah that a widow in Zarephath had been commanded to sustain him. That may have come as a shock to you since you did not have enough to sustain your child and yourself.

Well, there you were at the city gate gathering a few spindly little sticks to make a cook fire, when who should show up but Elijah. He was thirsty and hungry. What were you supposed to do about that? Soon it became abundantly clear. He called to you, "Hey, lady. Bring me a cup of water, please." Just like a man. You might have told him, "Get it yourself. I'm not your slave and I'm not your wife." Then, you must have remembered God's command which was, no doubt, more compelling than Elijah's. So, off you went to fetch the water. Before you took three steps, Elijah shouted again, "And bring me some bread." That was when you explained to him your financial predicament. "I don't have any bread to give you. In fact, I don't have any bread to give my child, never mind that I get hungry, too. As a matter of fact, I was just getting ready to take the last little handful of flour I have and mix it with the last of the oil. I was gathering sticks to make a fire so I could prepare the last meal my child and I would eat. After that, we would just wait to die."

Elijah gave you a comforting word, some instructions, and some good news. First, "Don't be afraid." Then, "Go make bread from what you have." And finally, "The Lord God of Israel will keep flour in your barrel and oil in your jug until the rains come and the drought is over." That's exactly what happened.

But there is more to your story. Your child died. Of course, under the circumstances you could hardly be held responsible for what you said to Elijah. "Did you come here to remind me of my sins?" What sins? What sort of old baggage had you been carrying and for how long? Having committed some unnamed sin, did you live in guilt and fear that God would eventually punish you? You leveled a terrible accusation at the prophet: "You killed my son." Elijah took your child's body to his room upstairs and prayed for the restoration of his life. Not until Elijah returned your child to you alive were you able to say, "Now I know you are a man of God." Was it not enough that God had miraculously supplied you with oil and flour all those days? How many miracles did it take to make a believer of you? Did you require that someone who was clearly dead come back to life? I suppose I should not accuse you. You ultimately did recognize Elijah as a man of God. And as for someone's being dead and then alive again, who in all this world would believe such a thing? I'll name you Jessica.

Jessica—feminine of Jesse—Hebrew "God exists"

REFLECTING

Have you ever worried about not being able to pay your bills?

Have you ever missed a meal because you did not have money to buy food?

How have you weathered the stress in times of scarcity?

How has your faith in God sustained you?

Do you believe God still works miracles?

Do you have difficulty believing in God's power?

THE TRUTHFUL HARLOT

At Gibeon the Lord appeared to Solomon during the night in a dream, and God said, "Ask for whatever you want me to give you."

I Kings 3:5

"So give your servant a discerning heart to govern your people and to distinguish between right and wrong. For who is able to govern this great people of yours?"

I Kings 3:9

Then the king gave his ruling: "Give the living baby to the first woman. Do not kill him; she is his mother."

I Kings 3:27

Dear Young Woman,

YOU CAUGHT KING SOLOMON AT a good time. He had just had a dream in which God told him to ask for whatever he wanted and it would be granted. Can you imagine! Solomon could have requested all the riches of the world. But he didn't. That which he requested pleased God. "Give me an understanding heart so I can judge the people and know what is good and what is bad." When Solomon woke from his dream, he went to Jerusalem and presented burnt offerings to the Lord before the Ark of the Covenant.

The smoke from the sacrifice had barely cleared when you and the other new mother came into King Solomon's presence. You asked him to adjudicate your case. The story you told was of a dead child. The woman who came with you had borne a child three days after your baby was born. Her baby suffocated in the bed with his mother when she inadvertently rolled over on him. Instead of crying out, she came to your room, made sure you were sleeping soundly, and switched babies. She took your living boy and put her dead child next to you. When morning came, you reached for the baby to nurse him and discovered, to your horror, a cold, lifeless little body. You immediately knew the dead child was not yours. When you saw that the other woman had your baby, you knew what she had done.

When you appeared before King Solomon, it soon became a "Did not," "Did, too," sort of interchange with your word against hers. Your blood must have run cold when the king offered a solution: "Bring a sword. Cut the child down the middle and each mom can have half." Your adversary quickly agreed that this was a great idea. You, on the other hand, immediately reacted by saying, "No, just give the baby to her." Solomon wisely (how else?) ruled that you were the true mother. No genius was needed to figure that one out. But the response of the populace was immediate. Solomon's fame spread throughout the kingdom. He was hailed as the wise king. Everyone said that he was guided by the Lord.

I hope that you, like Solomon, acquired wisdom along the way. And I hope that you learned to ask the Lord for guidance. Did life ever get better for you? Did you move out of that house of ill repute? Did you find better work? Did your boy grow up to be an honorable man? Did you ever tell him how close he came to being sliced down the middle? I also wonder what happened to the woman who tried to steal your baby. I wish her well. Life was not easy for either one of you, but you did, ultimately, get to keep your baby. She lost hers. I hope she became a follower of the one true God because in Him we find compassion for our humanity, mercy for our failures, and comfort for our sorrows. I'll name you Felicity because Solomon gave you back your child.

Felicity—Hebrew "good fortune"

REFLECTING

If God told you that you could have anything you want, what would you request?

What do you understand about wisdom?

Do you believe wisdom comes automatically with age?

Have you had the experience of:
- being lied to?
- having something valuable stolen from you?
- being vindicated?

Do you believe God punishes all sin and rewards all good behavior?

ABIGAIL'S FIVE MAIDS

A certain man in Maon, who had property there at Carmel, was very wealthy. He had a thousand goats and three thousand sheep, which he was shearing in Carmel. His name was Nabal and his wife's name was Abigail. She was an intelligent and beautiful woman, but her husband. . .was surly and mean in his dealings.

I Samuel 25:2–3

David said to Abigail, "Praise be to the Lord, the God of Israel, who has sent you today to meet me. May you be blessed for your good judgment and for keeping me from bloodshed this day and from avenging myself with my own hands."

I Samuel 25:32–33

When David heard that Nabal was dead, he said, "Praise be to the Lord, who has upheld my cause against Nabal for treating me with contempt.

I Samuel 25:39

Abigail quickly got on a donkey and, attended by her five maids, went with David's messengers and became his wife.

I Samuel 25:42

Dear Five Maids,

HOW DOES ONE GET TO be the maid of someone like Abigail? Your relationship with her can be chalked up either to God's blessing or random luck. I'm guessing that Abigail was a blessing to you. She might have been just another beautiful rich woman, an ornament on her husband's arm. But your mistress was someone special. As you worked for her, you, no doubt, observed that she was not only beautiful and intelligent, but also wise and kind. How can it be that this lovely woman was married to Nabal? I'm sure you had ample opportunity to observe their marriage. If Nabal treated Abigail the way he treated David, she might have spent much of her marriage weeping in misery. I do not think that happened. I think Abigail, trapped as she was, simply decided that she would have a healthy and productive life, even though she married a stingy, surly, and, no doubt, controlling man.

I imagine that you five servant girls found the situation highly instructive. You must have loved and admired Abigail. Did you ever feel sorry for her because she was married to Nabal? Would it not have been much better if she had married a man worthy of her? Did you admire her for her wisdom and courage and for her belief in the Lord God? Abigail was wise to have managed a bad situation so skillfully.

When she heard that Nabal had insulted David—not the first time he had offended someone—Abigail decided not to tell her husband what she had in mind to do. She took matters into her own capable hands. With great courage, she met David and four hundred of his armed men. She offered a peace offering, assumed responsibility for the insults, and convinced David not to shed innocent blood. When Abigail returned home, she found her husband at a party, drunk. Wisely, she waited until the next morning, when he was sober, to tell him all that had occurred. Could anyone have foreseen that Nabal, upon hearing the news, would suffer a heart attack? Ten days later, he was dead. David, crediting God with Nabal's demise, lost no time in proposing matrimony to the freshly widowed Abigail. She might have put him off for a while, if for no other reason than to enjoy her newly found freedom, but she did not. Abigail bowed down her face to the ground and promised to wash the feet of David's servants. She may have overdone the humility bit just a tad, but never mind. She gathered up the five of you, her faithful servants, and, with David's men, headed to the wedding chapel. I wonder if the five of you had matching outfits, carried little bouquets, and served as Abigail's bridesmaids? I'm sure it was a lovely wedding.

Not to take the joy out of the occasion, but scripture adds, almost as an afterthought: "David also married Ahinoam from Jezreel. They were both his wives." Men! Do you believe it? Ultimately, David married eight times, and he had, in addition, what one little boy of my acquaintance called many "porcupines." I don't know how women in your culture could tolerate that behavior. In my century, women would rebel.

All things considered, Abigail demonstrated wisdom in her submission, perhaps the only survival mechanism available to her. She understood what was required.

What shall I name the five of you? I know! Dulce, Dorothy, Darlene, Drusilla, and Dorcas.

Dulce—Latin "dulcis"—sweet
Dorothy—Greek "dorotheus"—gift of God
Darlene—Old English "deorling" darling
Drusilla—Latin "drusus" strong
Dorcas—Greek "gazelle" graceful

REFLECTING

Have you ever known anyone who was consistently negative?

Do you know anyone who must blame someone else for what goes wrong?

On the contrary, do you know someone who assumes blame for something for which they are not responsible?

Is there such a thing as being "too nice"?

What is the difference in taking a stand and being "mean"?

What do you believe about the person who is, always is the one to apologize after a conflict?

THE FORGOTTEN CONCUBINE

"The man took his concubine and sent her outside to them, and they raped her and abused her throughout the night, and at dawn they let her go. At daybreak the woman went back to the house where her master was staying, fell down at the door and lay there until daylight. When her master got up in the morning and opened the door of the house and stepped out to continue on his way, there lay his concubine, fallen in the doorway of the house, with her hands on the threshold. He said to her, 'Get up; let's go.' But there was no answer. Then the man put her on his donkey and set out for home. When he reached home, he took a knife and cut up his concubine, limb by limb, into twelve parts and sent them into all the areas of Israel."

Judges 19:25b–29

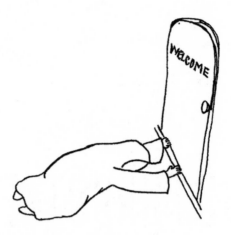

Dear abused and murdered woman,

WORDS FAIL ME WHEN I read your story. I can only feel revulsion, horror, and rage. You were bought and sold, an early victim of sexual abuse and torture. You managed to escape and return to your father. You stayed with him four months. And when your owner came to reclaim you, the two men had a merry time together. They must have spoken the same male language and had a lot to say to each other. Where were you during this time of eating and drinking and general merrymaking? What were you thinking? I suppose it doesn't really matter. Throughout this narrative you were utterly helpless, irrelevant, cast aside. According to the scriptural account, you never spoke—not one word.

When finally your master decided to leave your father's house, he had with him his male attendant, two donkeys, and you, in that order. The three of you journeyed through the day. The sun set. Danger lurked. The two men (your master and his attendant) decided to bypass Jerusalem and spend the night in Gibeah. Of course, no one asked your opinion on the matter. They wouldn't, would they? You found yourselves in the public square in that city where no one offered hospitality until an old man appeared and struck up a conversation with your master. Shocked at the very idea that you were planning to spend the night on the city streets, he took all of you to his home and there offered you food and shelter.

Just as you were settling in, a mob from the city surrounded the house, beat on the door, and shouted for the old man to throw out your master so they could sexually abuse him. The old man refused and offered them his virgin daughter and you. He said, "Do whatever you like with them, but don't do any 'vile thing' (KJV) to the man." At that point the virgin daughter and her father disappear from the story. Your master shoved you out the door and into the crazed mob. You were gang-raped "all night long until morning." And you were tortured. Finally, they let you go. You dragged yourself to the doorway of the old man's house where you fell and managed to grab the threshold with both hands. When I think of you bleeding, beaten, perhaps already dead, my heart hurts for you and all the women abused through the centuries.

In the morning when your master found you, he showed no compassion. "Come on; get up. Let's get on the road." Were you already dead? He picked you up and slung you onto the back of a donkey, and when you arrived at his house, he took the knife and cut your body into twelve pieces. He sent pieces of your body throughout Israel, a call for revenge for what was done to HIM, the rape, torture, and destruction of his property. The next two chapters of Judges tell of the massive carnage that followed.

What happened to you is appalling, disturbing, horrific. Your ancient story still unfolds in my century. Can you believe it? Women are still raped and murdered. Children are sold as sex slaves. Human trafficking is a billion-dollar industry in my world. Can you fathom the fact that evil still flourishes to this extent? Can you think why on earth humanity has not progressed beyond this abomination four thousand years after you lived a life of misery and died at the hands of evil men?

To you who had no voice, I can only offer words of pity—a poor offering indeed.

To you who had no name, I can give you a name which epitomizes what your master thought of you. It is a name which evildoers use to define all victims of abuse: I'll name you Nadia, from the Spanish "nada" which means "nothing." I give it because you were "no thing." You were a living, breathing woman who did not deserve despicable treatment at the hands of evil men.

REFLECTING

How do you react to news of another woman raped, another child sexually abused?

Why does God not intervene in the face of such evil?

What historical events does this story call to your mind?

Why is the period of the judges so full of carnage?

Do you think such things are still happening in our world today?

Do you agree that there is nothing new under the sun?

THE SISTER OF PAUL

The Jews formed a conspiracy and bound themselves with an oath not to eat or drink until they had killed Paul.

Acts 23:12

But when the son of Paul's sister heard of this plot, he went into the barracks and told Paul. Then Paul called one of the centurions and said, "Take this young man to the commander, he has something to tell him."

Acts 23:17

Dear Sister of Paul,

I WISH I KNEW MORE about you. There is only one oblique reference to you in Luke's history of the early church. He writes that more than forty Jewish men agreed they would not eat nor drink anything until they had killed your brother, Paul. We are not told exactly how your son heard that his Uncle Paul was in danger from these men, nor are we told your name, nor the name of your son. All we know is that Paul's life was spared due to your son's courage and wisdom. Your child knew what to do; he cast fear aside and bravely took action. I have to wonder if his actions stemmed from the upbringing he received from his exemplary parents. You and his father have every reason to be proud of this young man.

Everyone who has ever heard of the Apostle Paul would be glad to know more about him. I wish I could talk to you about him. Was your brother always a high achiever? I assume so. His Greek is both polished and convoluted. Of course, his education was the best your culture had to offer, beyond comparison. Do you remember when the two of you were children? Your brother was called Saul in those days. Do you remember when he sat at the feet of his teacher, Gamaliel? Like every Jewish male, he began early to memorize long passages of scripture. Did you think that Saul would one day rise to become a Pharisee of the Pharisees? What a remarkable mind he had.

All the time Saul was learning the Law, you, like most Jewish girls of your time, no doubt, were learning how to be a good and frugal wife and mother. I wonder if you also had a bright, inquiring mind. If you never did a thing but produce that fine son, you made an indelible mark on history.

Saul started out so adamantly against the sect that had grown up around the man, Jesus of Nazareth, and he dragged many of the followers into prison. Your brother was absolutely convinced that this sect was detrimental to the Jews' one true God. Saul was present and active at the stoning of Stephen. He was certain that in wiping out the apostate believers, he was doing God's work. I wonder if, even after his conversion, your brother resolved his remorse for those actions. Without a doubt, he considered himself chief of sinners who had been saved by the grace of God through the shed blood of Jesus. Still, one can never go back and undo dreadful things. Saul's motives were pure. He thought he was doing right. Did he ever talk to you about any of this? Did you ever initiate a conversation about it? I think of all he went through for his faith—persecution, shipwreck, imprisonment, death. I hope you had opportunity to be with your brother when he was in Rome. His execution was such a shock. I can only imagine how dreadful it must have been for you and the rest of his family. Thank God for His promise of resurrection.

I thank God for your brother. His letters make up a large portion of our holy book. I wonder if he came to you from time to time for comfort and encouragement. You were his sister, after all. I'm naming you Christina.

Christina—feminine form of Christian—Greek "kristos"—anointed one

REFLECTING

How have people in your life influenced you for good?

In your family, were both girls and boys given the same educational opportunities?

Did you have a sibling with whom you shared a deep friendship?

What do you treasure most about that relationship?

Have you ever made a decision which changed all the rest of your life?

Has anyone ever rescued you? How is that intervention a part of your life story?

There is one Redeemer —with a capital R—and many redeemers— with a lower case r. Who has been a help to you in times of trouble?

THE WISE WOMAN OF TEKOA

*Joab, son of Zeruiah knew that the king's heart longed for
Absalom. So Joab sent someone to Tekoa and had a wise
woman brought from there. He said to her, "Pretend you are
in mourning. Dress in mourning clothes, and don't use any
cosmetic lotions. Act like a woman who has spent many days
grieving for the dead. Then go to the king and speak these
words to him. And Joab put the words in her mouth."*
II Samuel 14:1–3

*The king said to Joab, "Very well. I will do it. Go, bring back
the young man, Absalom. Joab fell with his face to the ground
to pay him honor, and he blessed the king."*
II Samuel 14:21–22

Dear Wise Woman,

YOU WERE FAMOUS FOR YOUR wisdom. I don't know what you did to impress Joab, but when he wanted King David to bring Absalom home from exile, you were the one to whom he turned for help. Joab had influence over the king, and David needed all the help he could get. He was a veritable magnet for trouble.

I don't know if you knew the history behind Joab's request to you. David was angry at Absalom for killing his brother, Amnon, who had raped their sister, Tamar. Talk about a dysfunctional family! Absalom had been in exile for three years, and Joab believed that Israel needed him to return as crown prince, the successor to the throne.

I doubt the convoluted history had any relevance for you. Joab just wanted you to be part of a ruse to get the king to send for his son. He gave you your "lines," and you turned out to be quite an outstanding actress. You gave an Academy Award performance before King David.

"Oh King David," you cried (dabbing at your eyes). "I had two sons and one of them killed the other."

At this point David might have said, "Hum, what a coincidence. This lady's story sounds just like what is going on in my own family." But he did not.

You played your part well, and David promised to help you. He relented enough also to promise he would send for Absalom, but not before he asked you, "Did Joab, by any chance, have anything to do with your little drama?"

You were wise enough to say something like, "Oh, you wonderful king! Aren't you just about the smartest thing God ever created! You have wisdom like the angel of God. No one can put anything over on you. Yes, I must admit that it was Joab who told me to dress up like a poor, grieving mother and come before you with the story he had concocted."

As it happened, David did reluctantly let Absalom come back home, but, as later history was to prove, the king's troubles with this son had only just begun. I will name you Angela. You are no angel, but you were the messenger of Joab.

Angela—Greek "angelos" angel or messenger

REFLECTING

Are there any unhealed wounds in your family of origin?

Do you have siblings? What is your relationship with them?

How has birth order among your siblings affected your relationships?

Complete these sentences:

Firstborn children are usually_____.

Middle children_____.

The baby of the family_____.

If you are an only child, you_____.

Is there someone in your family whom you need to forgive?

Is there a member of your family to whom you need to apologize?

COMPANION OF CLEOPAS

Now that same day two of them were going to a village called Emmaus, about seven miles from Jerusalem. They were talking with each other about everything that had happened. As they talked and discussed these things with each other, Jesus himself came up and walked along with them, but they were kept from recognizing him.

Luke 24:13–16

Afterward Jesus appeared in a different form to two of them while they were walking in the country. These returned and reported it to the rest; but they did not believe them.

Mark 16:12–13

Near the cross of Jesus stood his mother, his mother's sister, Mary the wife of Cleopas, and Mary Magdalene.

John 19:25

Dear Believer,

MEN ARE OFTEN NAMED IN the same biblical passage with a woman who remains unnamed—Job and Peter, but not their wives; Samson and Jabez, but not their mothers; the brothers of Jesus, but not their sisters; the twelve disciples, but not the "many other women" who followed him from Galilee. Neither Mark nor Luke names the person who, with Cleopas, left Jerusalem that first day of the week. In fact, Mark doesn't name Cleopas either. We know that after the women found the tomb empty, Cleopas and an unnamed companion went to Emmaus. It has been assumed by most readers of scripture that it was a man who accompanied Cleopas, but there are now women theologians who are asking if it might have been a woman.

Luke gives the more detailed account: you and Cleopas were walking toward Emmaus, talking about all the events of the last week. You were, no doubt, weeping with grief. Jesus came to walk with you, but you did not recognize him. He asked what you had been talking about, and, so typical of him, he asked why you were so sad. Cleopas responded with some measure of surprise. "You must be a stranger in town." It was the sort of answer that said, "Unless you were trapped in the bottom of a mine shaft last week, you would know." Or, "Good heavens, we thought everyone knew about the crucifixion of Jesus!" Or, "Don't you read the Jerusalem newspapers?" Since the stranger didn't seem to know what was going on in the world, Cleopas explained. "Jesus was a mighty prophet," he said. "We thought he was the Messiah. This is the third day after his crucifixion." Then he added, "Certain women of our company astonished us. They were first at the tomb. They saw angels, but they did not find his body. It was not there." Some of the men finally decided to check out their story, and, by heaven, it turned out to be true after all."

The stranger's response was immediate: "Dimwits! You don't get it, do you? Didn't all the prophets predict just such a thing? You should know that Christ had to suffer all these things before he entered into his glory." And then you and Cleopas were treated to the best Bible study anyone could ever imagine, taught by the Son of God Himself. From Moses and all the prophets this stranger expounded on the scriptures.

By the time you got to Emmaus, seven miles from Jerusalem, the sun was setting. The man with you appeared to be going on down the road, but you insisted that he come into the house. I am assuming you had arrived at your own home. I wonder if you were the one who invited him in for a meal. You settled yourselves around the table. The stranger blessed and broke the bread. Instantly, you and Cleopas knew that you were in the presence of the Lord. The moment you recognized Him, He vanished from your sight. You said to each other, "We should have known who it was with whom we spent the afternoon. Did our hearts not burn within us as He taught us from the scriptures?" So, as fast as your legs could carry you, you and Cleopas retraced your steps. Breathlessly, you returned to Jerusalem. A fourteen-mile hike would ordinarily leave most people exhausted, but the two of you were propelled by adrenalin. You could not wait to tell the others. "We have seen Him! He is risen!"

I don't have to name you. I believe your name is Mary. I believe you were one of the six Marys in the gospels. John mentions your presence at the cross: "Near the cross of Jesus stood his mother, his mother's sister, Mary the wife of Cleopas, and Mary Magdalene." I believe it was you who went with Cleopas from Jerusalem to Emmaus and back again. I believe it was you who walked with Jesus that day. If not, Cleopas was with someone else. And we are left with the question: why would Cleopas go to Emmaus and leave his wife in Jerusalem? It is something to think about.

REFLECTING

Why do we so easily accept the prevailing assumptions about scripture?

Is it wrong to question "what we always thought" about stories in the Bible?

Might our spiritual vision be enhanced by looking at familiar stories from a different point of view?

If you had been on the road to Emmaus, do you think you might have recognized Jesus?

AFTERWORD

WHY BOTHER TO NAME ALL of the women in this study? What does it matter, after all? Without a name, a person lacks identity and stories lose reality. How can we think of the Christmas story without Mary? When Magdalene was seeking Jesus at the tomb, she did not recognize Him until He called her name. When Paul wrote to the various first century churches, he took care to call the names of specific people in the congregations. That inclusion of names created characters to enact the work of the church.

Even children know the joy that comes in hearing their names called by a loved teacher, by their school principal, by their pastor. Adults do not outgrow the need to hear their names called. Name-sharing is the first step in knowing another person. Strangers become friends by first offering this primary information about themselves.

Naming the unnamed women in scripture confers upon them deserved dignity and identity. They gain position and a place not proffered by their culture. The power that comes with naming grants inclusion and a new citizenship in the biblical story.

Characters in the Old Testament looked forward in faith. Those in the New Testament looked back for history. The nexus of encounter for both is the Cross and the Resurrection. With names, the unnamed women have a part in the big story.

The words of this study were written, recalling Paul's words about Jesus:

> *"God has highly exalted him, and given him a name which is above every name, that at the name of Jesus every knee should bow, of things in heaven, and things on earth, and things under the earth; and that every tongue confess that Jesus Christ is Lord to the glory of God the Father."*
>
> *Philippians 2:10–11*

ACKNOWLEDGEMENTS

MY ABIDING GRATITUDE TO:
Professor Gladys Sherman Lewis, heart friend of sixty years, who invited me to her Oklahoma home and spent hours discussing and editing this little volume;

Rick Bates, infinitely patient guide through the publishing process;

The Jim Williams Sunday School class at Chester Baptist Church, for listening to each sketch as it was being written and laughed in all the right places;

Dr. Jim Somerville, pastor of First Baptist Church, Richmond, Virginia—my friend who knows how to use the English language, how to encourage, and how to love as Jesus loves;

Dr. Lloyd Braswell, my pastor, who meets every crisis with grace and took precious time out to listen to me read about unnamed women of the Bible;

Patricia Jones, good friend and spiritual benefactor, who reads everything I write and prays for me every day;

Deborah Edgar, who got teary-eyed over the Woman at the Well;

Bernice Rodgerson, who reads and reacts with delight;

Sandra Bollinger, who laughed over Mrs. Noah when I forced her to listen to that chapter.

Janet Chase, who pointed me to a publisher with all good wishes for success;

My friend Bev Carroll, who knows her Bible, provides me inspiration, and also writes books;

Dr. Ron Dubois, friend and mentor, who often says, "When are you going to write another book?"

Don and Mary McBride, my brother and sister-in-law, who have always loved me and anything I write;

My cousins Betty Paxton and Kathy Beasley who listened and laughed;

My cousin, Suzanne Saunders, who suggested the final title when I complained that the working title was as dull as dishwater;

And finally, thanks to the rest of my family, with particular gratitude to my artistic granddaughter, Melissa Damon, who created the illustrations, and my husband, Bill Damon, official technical guru, who endures much.

ABOUT THE AUTHOR

ROBERTA MCBRIDE DAMON GREW UP in Oklahoma and Virginia. She graduated from Mars Hill College and Oklahoma Baptist University and did graduate work at the University of Maryland and Southwestern Baptist Theological Seminary. She and her husband, Bill, served as Southern Baptist missionaries to Brazil in their early years. Upon returning to the States, Roberta went back to Southwestern and earned her master's degree and her doctorate in marriage and family therapy. She served on staff of First Baptist Church, Richmond, Virginia, as a marriage and family counselor and, after her "retirement," as staff counselor for the International Mission Board of the Southern Baptist Convention. Her former publications include her memoir, *A Voice Beyond Weeping*, and a fictionalized account of the early church in Rome, *Theirs is the Kingdom*. She is mother of two sons and grandmother of three delightful grandchildren.

WORKS CONSULTED

Barclay, William. *The Gospel of Matthew*. The Westminster Press, Philadelphia, 1956.

————————-*The Gospel of Mark*. The Westminster Press, Philadelphia, 1954.

————————-*The Gospel of Luke*. The Westminster Press, Philadelphia, 1953.

The Comparative Study Bible, New International Version. Zondervan, Grand Rapids, Michigan, 1984.

Editors, *Consumer Guide*. *The Ultimate Baby Name Book*. Publications International, Ltd., Lincolnwood, Illinois, 1994.

Smith, William. *Smith's Bible Dictionary*. A. J. Holman Company, Philadelphia, no date.